The Reference Information Skills Game

The Reference Information Skills Game

MYRAM FORNEY TUNNICLIFF

SUSAN SHELDON SOENEN

1995
LIBRARIES UNLIMITED, INC.
Englewood, Colorado

LIBRARIES UNLIMITED, INC.
P.O. Box 6633
Englewood, CO 80155-6633
1-800-237-6124

Project Editor: Tama J. Serfoss
Copy Editor: Tama J. Serfoss
Proofreader: Eileen Bartlett
Layout: Kay Minnis

Library of Congress Cataloging-in-Publication Data

Tunnicliff, Myram Forney.
The reference information skills game / Myram Forney Tunnicliff, Susan Sheldon Soenen.
xvi, 107 p. 22x28 cm.
Includes index.
ISBN 1-56308-296-9
1. Libraries—United States—Problems, exercises, etc.
2. Reference books—Problems, exercises, etc. 3. Educational games—United States. I. Soenen, Susan Sheldon. II. Title.
Z710.T86 1995
025.5'24'076—dc20 94-49401
CIP

Contents

Acknowledgments

We would like to acknowledge the great assistance given to us by David V. Loertscher, Vice President Editorial/Production at Libraries Unlimited. Thank you!

We're grateful, also, to Linda Twait, Librarian, and Jenifer Thayer, English teacher, who tested The Reference Information Skills Game in their libraries and classroom.

And to Dick Tunnicliff, who did everything from proofread to cook the dinner, another big thank you.

Introduction

While watching the fumbling attempts of community college students endeavoring to locate answers to factual reference questions, we became convinced that a new approach to teaching library skills was needed in elementary and high school. These community college students seemed to have no method to their searching, but we knew that they had been taught library units in their schools. What methods would equip these young people to deal with and benefit from the growing mounds of information available to them? What methods would teach a "process" for finding information more effectively than the commonly used browse/accidental approach? We decided to come up with an approach that would teach middle and secondary students some generic information retrieval methods and yet be one that students would enjoy and use daily.

The Reference Information Skills Game has been used successfully at both a middle school (grades 5-8) and a K-12 media center and will be equally effective in a public library setting. It has been used in library media centers and in classrooms in which library units were presented.

The basic idea of the game is to take one aspect of information skills—fact location—and turn it into a fun game in which analyzing the process of finding information is as important as actually locating the fact. Many library science students are familiar with the technique of using fact location to become familiar with reference materials. The difference here is that students soon learn that process counts as much as product. As they do this, patterns of searching begin to emerge, replacing the random hunting methods employed in the past. The game has been structured so that students soon realize that there is more than one way to locate information and that a successful searcher must be flexible and clever as the process develops.

To play the game, the teacher or library media specialist posts a question on a bulletin board with a catchy clue. Every day, a new clue is added, the clues getting progressively easier as the game week progresses. Students win the game when they successfully solve the question. They must submit not only the correct answer but also a search map that demonstrates the process through which they found the answer. In addition to gaining experience in the library media center and the classroom, the students learn the life-long skill of problem solving.

The weekly question contests cover a large range of topics, all chosen to appeal to the students' interests. Not only do students learn new and interesting facts, but in the process of finding the answers, they also learn about other topics they encounter while researching. They are also encouraged to be on the lookout for conflicting information and are rewarded for making quality judgments.

This book presents 162 prepared questions complete with clues for the busy librarian and classroom teacher, but after a few experiences, you will probably want to create questions and clues on your own. Young people may also be encouraged to create questions and clues. Using the subject index at the end of the book, game questions can be chosen to integrate into topical units of instruction being studied in the classroom, or one class might write questions based on a topical unit of study and challenge another class to answer them—and vice versa.

Once the game is over, and especially if the class has been challenged by the question, it is important to debrief the class. What sources contained the best information? What were the best search strategies to use? What strategies saved the most time? Why were conflicting answers found and how was the conflict resolved? Was the conflict resolved? What are the most useful aids within a reference tool to help the user find information quickly (e.g., tables of contents, indexes, text structure)? If electronic reference tools were used, what strategies helped in locating the information quickly?

SPECIFICS OF THE GAME

"Solve our mystery question, and get your name up in 'lights'."

That's the challenge of The Reference Information Skills Game, an educational activity used to encourage the use of resource materials, as it has been played in the Emmetsburg, Iowa, middle school and in the Mallard, Iowa, K-12 library. In a prominent spot in a classroom or library, a question is posted with one fairly difficult clue. On each succeeding day, another clue is added giving information that is progressively easier to find in the print materials and through audiovisual, computer, and human sources. A student may not simply guess the answer but must have a resource in hand to prove that the answer was researched. Some teachers may want to have students use the information that they have found to write a report or create a project.

Have students record their search process on the reproducible Reference Information Skills Game Search Map found at the end of this section (see the handout on pages xv-xvi). As the students move from resource to resource, have them show their research process on the map using arrows to indicate the areas they have explored and make notes by the arrows about their search strategy and what they have found (see fig. 1, p. xi, for a sample map). Have students record the titles of the sources they consult and note any conflicting information or misinformation they find. Discuss with the students how to make quality judgments in choosing their answers. Teachers may want to give extra credit to students who are able to defend their decisions regarding conflicting information.

As students answer the question, they turn in their completed search maps and verifying sources. The teacher or librarian can end the game and post the answer after one day of winners, or can keep the game going for a couple more days, providing more clues for students who need more time. Those who answered the question correctly get their names on the bulletin board next to the question. At the Emmetsburg Middle School, students who win the game get their names printed on light bulbs appropriately arranged under the heading "Lights." They now have their names up in lights. As an added incentive, winners get a badge of recognition with a light bulb and the words "Watt a Bright Kid!" (see fig. 2).

Fig. 2. Badge of recognition given at the Emmetsburg Middle School.

Page 1

The Reference Information Skills Game

Search Map

Name: Jane Anystudent

Directions: To show the research process you followed in finding the answer, draw arrows showing your search path and give the titles of the sources you have used. Make brief notes by your arrows explaining your thoughts as you followed your search path.

Question # 1 **Write question here:** Who stuffed paper into his telephone bell to prevent it from interrupting his work?

My Search Map

My mind (What I already know) — probably a man who lived in early days of telephone + probably an inventor

Encyclopedias — WORLD BOOK, AMERICANA — got frustrated

Dictionaries

Library Catalog — Couldn't find anything

Magazine Index

Vertical File

Atlases

Reference Books (not encyclopedias, dictionaries, or atlases)

CD-ROM Station

Biographies — Checked answer in "The Chord of Steel" by Thomas B. Costain

Nonfiction Books (not reference or biographies) — found answer in inventor book "Those Inventive Americans" by National Geographic Society

Expert Person

Page 2

My answer: Alexander Graham Bell

Source the answer was found in: Those Inventive Americans

Source the answer was verified in: The Chord of Steel

Other interesting facts I learned: He was one of the first believers in mechanical flight and experimented for years with box kites.

Strange things I noticed about the research process: The encyclopedia index wasn't very helpful in either one I used.

What I will do differently the next time I research: I'll try the index in other reference books besides encyclopedias.

Fig. 1. Sample search map.

RESEARCH STRATEGIES

Cooperation between the library media specialist and the classroom teacher in teaching research strategies makes the Reference Information Skills Game workable in a classroom setting. The teacher could make use of many of these questions at the beginning of a unit as a way to generate student interest in the subject. Questions could also be used at the end of a unit as a review or even as that unit's test!

An excellent way to go beyond the typical library skills curriculum and introduce library skills as a process in the classroom would be emphasis on the "Big Six Skills" as presented by Michael B. Eisenberg and Robert E. Berkowitz in their books *Curriculum Initiative: An Agenda and Strategy for Library Media Programs* (Ablex 1988) and *Information Problem-Solving* (Ablex 1990).

A short version of their research strategy includes:

1. I have an information problem. What is it?
2. Where are the best places to look for the answer?
3. Which library skills do I use to find the sources I need?
4. When I find some information, is it any good?
5. When I get good information, how will I communicate it?
6. If I had to do this search again, how would I do it differently?

A more lengthy version of the same process is as follows:

1. Define the question that needs to be answered and what informational needs have to be met to answer the problem.
2. Decide which available sources might fulfill this task. Consider text, audiovisual, computer, and human resources. It is important to point out to students that there may be more than one correct source, and urge them to compare resources and judge for themselves which fill their needs more satisfactorily.
3. Find the sources using traditional library skills. An excellent program for teaching sequential library skills can be found in *Teaching the Library Research Process* (The Center for Applied Research 1985) and *School Librarian's Grade-by-Grade Activities Program* (The Center for Applied Research 1981), both by Carol Collier Kuhlthau.
4. Decide what information that you have located is important and how to save it (taking notes, photocopying, and so on) for future use.
5. Combine and synthesize the information from the various materials into the accepted format as directed by the librarian or teacher, including the citing of sources.
6. Assess the final presentation or answer to see if it has come to a satisfactory conclusion and if the needs of the problem were met.

It is also important to stress to students that this process does not always have to follow the same sequence; it is a circular, nonlinear process. At any time in the research process, it may be necessary to go back to a previous step, to reevaluate new information, or try a new path. It is a good idea to have the search strategy steps on the back of the search map handout so that students are able to refer to it at any time during the game (see handout on pages xv-xvi).

The following example illustrates how this circular process could work in solving a question from the Reference Information Skills Game (note that this is question number 103 in the question and answer section):

Who stuffed paper into his telephone bell to prevent it from interrupting his work?

Step 1: You are trying to find a person who did this. You can gather that it is a male and he lived in earlier times when telephones were made differently than they are today. You determine that you need information concerning such an era and person.

First clue: He perfected a hydroplane.

Step 2: This tells you that you are looking for an inventor, so the range of resources would include encyclopedias, dictionaries, vertical file materials, and books and magazines on inventors and inventions, electronics, science, and aviation. A search of computer, audiovisual, and human sources is also indicated.

Step 3: As you follow through with your information-seeking skills using all aspects of the resource center, note on your search map the areas you have researched.

As the clues continue, you learn that the subject directed breeding experiments in sheep and also developed an electrical apparatus to locate bullets in the body in an effort to save President James Garfield's life. With these clues, you may want to go back to Steps 2 and 3 to redirect your search toward either agricultural or biographical and historical materials.

Step 4: Evaluate the information that you have located to determine what is important, how it relates to the clues, and what guidance it provides for further research.

Step 5: Using the needed clues (and it may take all of the clues), you consolidate all the information you have found and arrive at the answer, Alexander Graham Bell. Verify the answer and check that your research map is complete. Turn in your search map and a source to corroborate your answer.

Step 6: Evaluate your finished product and the process you used. Ask yourself if there may have been a more efficient way to arrive at the solution, and consider how you would do things differently in the future.

Once students use this form of problem solving successfully, they will find that it is a skill that can be used in all academic and life experience areas.

USING THE GAME TO TEACH LIBRARY SKILLS

The questions and clues in this book have been used successfully in school situations at all levels and are based on encyclopedias, print materials, CD-ROMs, audiovisuals, and magazines found in most libraries. The questions and clues have been classroom tested and have been proven to be highly motivational. They were formulated to appeal to a variety of interests and should help students develop a number of information skills in the pursuit of the answer.

As students become more comfortable with the process, interest and competition increase. We want this experience to be fun and challenging so that students will try hands-on work with a variety of reference materials and will use problem-solving techniques. The fun often comes from learning facts that have had nothing to do with the question that was first posted.

At the Emmetsburg Middle School, the Reference Information Skills Game, called Lights, is being used as described above, with students, teachers, and staff joining in the fun. It came as no surprise to the librarians that during the initial weeks of the game, the first choice of the students was encyclopedias. But as the quarter progressed, there was a definite increase in the number of sources students used. Often there were as many different sources as there were winners. In fact, some of the participants found the answers in sources that surprised the librarians! It has been interesting to note that winners have been children who are mentally challenged as well as honor students. If students feel that completing the research map is too much work, try oral questioning to encourage them to re-enter the challenge. At the end of the school year it is suggested the librarian reward the person who has been first with the answer the most times.

The librarian and the English teacher at the Emmetsburg Middle School work together to use the game to teach the fifth-grade library unit. It is particularly useful in introducing the library to the new fifth-graders who have never used the media center in that building before. The two instructors grade the search maps and finished reports. The librarian gives points for the ways the children use the library. The English teacher gives more credit for the substance learned (including conflicting information) and the presentation in their papers. But both emphasize to the students the idea that they are learning a problem-solving method that will be used lifelong.

REFERENCES

Eisenberg, Michael B., and Robert E. Berkowitz. "Curriculum Initiative: An Agenda and Strategy for Library Media Programs." Norwood, NJ: Ablex Publishing, 1988.

———. "Information Problem-Solving: The Big Six Skills Approach to Library and Information Skills Instruction." Norwood, NJ: Ablex Publishing, 1990.

Kuhlthau, Carol Collier. "School Librarian's Grade-by-Grade Activities Program: A Complete Sequential Skills Plan for Grades K-8." West Nyack, NY: The Center for Applied Research, 1981.

———. "Teaching the Library Research Process: A Step-by-Step Program for Secondary School Students." West Nyack, NY: The Center for Applied Research, 1985.

The Reference Information Skills Game

Search Map

Name:____

Directions: To show the research process you followed in finding the answer, draw arrows showing your search path and give the titles of the sources you have used. Make brief notes by your arrows explaining your thoughts as you followed your search path.

Question #__________ **Write question here:**__________________________________

____

____

My Search Map

My mind (What I already know)	Encyclopedias	Dictionaries
Library Catalog	Magazine Index	Vertical File
Atlases	Reference Books (not encyclopedias, dictionaries, or atlases)	CD-ROM Station
Biographies	Nonfiction Books (not reference or biographies)	Expert Person

My answer:____________________

Source the answer was found in:____________________

Source the answer was verified in:____________________

Other interesting facts I learned:____________________

____

Strange things I noticed about the research process:____________________

____

What I will do differently the next time I research:____________________

____

Search Strategy for Solving the Reference Information Skills Game

1. I have an information problem. What is it?
2. Where are the best places to look for the answer?
3. Which library skills do I use to find the sources I need?
4. When I find some information, is it any good?
5. When I get good information, how will I communicate it?
6. If I had to do this search again, how would I do it differently?

The above suggestions are loosely based on Michael B. Eisenberg and Robert E. Berkowitz's "Big Six Skills" as presented in their book *Information Problem-Solving* (Ablex 1990).

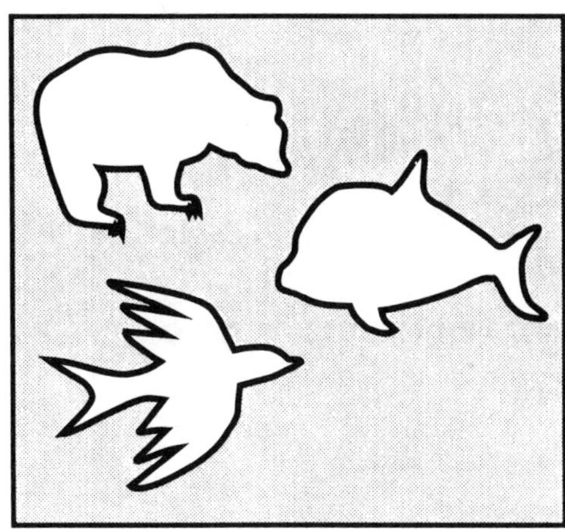

Animals

Amphibians

1

What uses its eyes to help itself swallow?

Clues:

- In dim light its pupils are oval; in the sun they contract to diamonds.
- It was believed to cure fevers, stop nosebleeds, dry up dropsy, keep rats away, sour the wine, milk the cows, rob birds' nests, and cause warts.
- It can be found everywhere except the polar regions, Australia, Madagascar, and a few islands.
- Only the male sings.
- It has been singing since before the first bird flew or the first flowers blossomed.
- One female may lay as many as 12,000 eggs.
- Its digestive system is born purely vegetarian, but becomes purely insectivorous.
- It never drinks; it sits in a puddle and absorbs moisture through the skin.

Answer: Toad

Aquatic Animals

2

What male animal has a pouch on its abdomen into which the female places eggs for hatching?

Clues:

- It has a toothless mouth.
- It's capable of a variety of color changes.
- It has a prehensile tail.
- Its diet consists of plankton.
- Its head is sometimes preserved, put on a base, and used as a chessman.
- It moves about in an upright position.
- One of its names, *Hippocampus*, comes from Greek words meaning "horse" and "bent."

Answer: Sea horse

3

What organism inhabits all the world's oceans and many freshwater streams, ponds, and lakes?

Clues:

- They have survived unchanged for hundreds of millions of years.
- Their colors range from subtle pastels to blazing reds, yellows, and blues.
- They have been used to make significant contributions to medicine. Doctors use one species to combat leukemia.
- They do not possess hearts, lungs, brains, or nervous systems and have no means of defense.
- Many marine species are immune to bacterial infection.
- Some are as small as beans and others are six feet or more.
- Today, industry uses them as a polisher.
- They can reproduce by regeneration as well as sexually.
- They can't move around, but live anchored to one spot.

Answer: Sponges

4

What invader from the Caspian Sea has in eight years since its arrival shut down a large utility and hampered the operations of other industries?

Clues:

- Its prolific reproductive habits have been said to "fall somewhere between those of rabbits and fruit flies."
- It threatens to restructure the ecology of the entire freshwater system in the United States.
- It is not much larger than a pistachio shell.
- It came to the United States in the hold of a ship along with water taken in as ballast and then disgorged on Lake St. Clair between Lakes Erie and Huron.
- Alternating stripes of white and brown account for its common name.
- It is a mollusk.
- Its Latin name is *Dreissena polymorpha* meaning "many forms."

Answer: Zebra mussel

Arachnids

5

What animal can have three or four pairs of legs, depending on its age?

Clues:

- Cases of paralysis are known to have followed its attack.
- It can sometimes survive for years without food.
- Females lay up to 8,000 eggs at a time.
- Its body is more or less oval.
- It is a parasite.
- One variety transmits lyme disease.
- Two kinds are best known for transmitting Rocky Mountain spotted fever.

Answer: Tick

Birds

6

What is a link with prehistoric times and earlier years in American history?

Clues:

- They have survived since Pleistocene times.
- They figure prominently in legends, dances, and religious ceremonies.
- They are believed to be able to survive a month without food.
- They lack the capacity to roost on branches.
- They can soar for an hour without flapping their wings.
- They're one of the largest birds on earth with a wingspread of nine feet.
- They lay only one egg per nesting attempt, but if that egg is lost, will often lay another.
- Their heads are orange-yellow and essentially bald.
- In an attempt to save them from extinction, all wild birds were captured for breeding purposes.
- The first birds bred in captivity were released in January of 1992.

Answer: California condors

7

What bird can easily kill a full-grown person?

Clues:

- It can grow to six feet tall and weigh 120 pounds.
- During World War II, Allied troops were sometimes attacked by these birds.
- It has been used to buy brides and pay debts.
- Its meat is dark colored and tastes more like beef than chicken.
- Each foot is three-toed, the inner toe being equipped with a sharp claw, four inches long.
- Although it can't fly, it can run fast, leap obstacles, and swim rivers.
- It is the largest native animal of New Guinea.
- Its head is crowned with a leathery "helmet" called a casque, which protects it when it runs through the jungle.

Answer: Cassowary

8

What bird doesn't build a nest?

Clues:

- It is known to have parasitized more than 150 species of birds (vireos, finches, fly-catchers, warblers, etc.) by leaving its eggs in the nests of other birds, relying on the foster parents to care for its young.
- The female lays four or five eggs each season, often in as many nests.
- Its incubation period is shorter than that of its foster siblings, so it may hatch a little sooner.
- The young are bigger than their foster siblings, so they hog the food supply.
- When the West was young, it was the constant companion of the buffalo.
- The male is about eight inches long with glossy black feathers except for its brown head and breast.
- When it grows weary of feeding on the ground, it rides on the back of a cow.

Answer: Cowbird

9

Which animal often kills its siblings in a "Cain and Abel" battle to the death?

Clues:

- Aristotle made one of the earliest known studies of them.
- The females are larger than males.
- They are found throughout the world except in the Antarctic.
- Their life span is usually 20-30 years, but can be more than 50 years.
- The young are hatched with eyes open.
- They were symbols of Roman warriors, Russian and Austrian emperors, and the United States.
- They can often carry their own body weight.
- Their feet and legs are their primary weapons.

Answer: Eagles

10

What bird is distantly related to geese and makes the same honking sounds?

Clues:

- Fossil forms have been found in France and Oregon.
- Once it learns to fly and can escape predators, it can look forward to a long life.
- It feeds with its head and bill upside down.
- It feeds its chick by drooling a red fluid that is 1 percent blood and is secreted from the lining of the throat.
- Most common among reasons for nesting failure are floods and droughts.
- The only breeding colony in the United States is at Hialeah racetrack in Florida.
- They have black wing quills and most are rosy white with scarlet shoulders, although the American variety is red.

Answer: Flamingo

11

What animal, when frightened, flattens itself to the ground and plays dead?

Clues:

- The female, when alarmed, sprays a rank-smelling oil.
- It was used as a hieroglyph in early Egypt.
- It lives in the temperate and tropic zones of Europe, Asia, and Africa.
- It is a favorite food in southern Europe.
- Its nest is so dirty, it can be located by its odor.
- It has a peculiar undulating manner of flying that displays to good advantage the black and white pattern of its wings and tail.
- It gets its name from its call which is a loud "hoop-hoop."

Answer: Hoopoe

12

What is the "king of song"?

Clues:

- It is called Cencontlatolly (400 tongues) by Indians.
- It is found from the Great Lakes south to the Gulf of Mexico and from South Dakota to Ontario and from Maine to California.
- Its wingbeats are slow enough to be counted.
- Northern migration began when farmers planted rose hedges instead of barbed wire fences.
- During its mating season, its serenade goes on for hours, day and night.
- It is pewter-colored and white-breasted.
- It is the state bird for five states
- It can sing its own song or the song of any bird it hears.

Answer: Mockingbird

13

What is the most abundant game bird in the United States?

Clues:

- Its population is approximately 500 million birds.
- More of these birds are harvested every year than all other migratory game birds combined.
- Thirty-two states permit hunting it.
- It is the only bird to keeps its bill in water while swallowing.
- It is a very poor nest builder.
- Two eggs per nest are most common.
- The young are fed on "milk," which is regurgitated food from their parents.
- Its legs are pink.

Answer: Mourning dove

14

What animal's name comes from the Latin word for "bonebreaker"?

Clues:

- It definitely gets its feet wet while fishing.
- The male eats the head of the fish for dinner and his mate then feeds the young and gets whatever is left over for herself.
- Some of the nests have enough material in them to fill a huge cart.
- It nests in trees, jagged rocks, low bushes, on the ground, and on the top of utility poles.
- It is about two feet long, with a wingspread of nearly six feet.
- The pesticide D.D.T. has endangered this animal, by causing fewer eggs to hatch.
- It is also called "fish hawk" and "fishing eagle."

Answer: Osprey

15

The term "stool pigeon" comes from the way these animals were hunted.

Clues:

- Its summer range extended from Nova Scotia and Central Quebec south to Kentucky and west to the eastern edge of the Great Plains, and it moved south to Florida, Arkansas, and Texas in the winter.
- It was about 16 or 17 inches in length including its long tapering tail.
- It often traveled 100 miles a day looking for food.
- Alexander Wilson reported a large flock in Kentucky he believed to number over 2 billion birds.
- A conservative guess as to how many were killed in 1878 at a single nesting area is 1½ million.
- By 1905, ornithological associations were offering rewards totaling $5,000 for information leading to the discovery of a nesting one of these.
- The sole survivor of the species died in a zoo in 1914.

Answer: Passenger pigeon

16

What animals “fly” through the water?

Clues:

- Fossils show they were flourishing in the same area 50 million years ago as they are now.
- They can swim at speeds of more than 16 knots for long stretches.
- To get from the sea onto land they can leap four to six feet into the air.
- Their wings are covered with plumage that feels more like scales than feathers.
- They can only take food underwater. Those kept in zoos must first be force-fed and then taught to pick up fish on land.
- They live in the Southern Hemisphere.
- They range in size from only one foot high to four-feet-tall species that weigh close to 100 pounds.
- Two species incubate the single egg by rolling it onto the male’s feet, where he keeps it warm by covering it with the lower part of his belly.

Answer: Penguins

17

What has been estimated to fly as fast as 250 mph?

Clues:

- Its diving for food is called “stooping.”
- It is the first choice of falconers.
- It has a distinctive dark mustache.
- Its numbers were significantly reduced in the 1950s and 1960s by pesticides.
- Those that are tundra-breeding migrate between northern North America and southern South America.
- It measures up to 20 inches long.
- It is being reintroduced into many of its present and former habitats, including a number of large cities.
- In North America it is sometimes called a duck hawk.

Answer: Peregrine falcon

18

What is often considered the herald of spring?

Clues:

- For more than 2,000 years, Greek children have sung songs to welcome them back in the spring.
- Their feet are tiny and weak.
- They have bills fringed with bristles to trap food.
- They are found worldwide except for polar regions.
- They feed on the wing.
- They normally eat insects, but if caught in the cold with no insects, they will eat bayberries.
- One variety of this family has one of the longest migration routes of American land birds.
- Indians hung rows of gourds on tall poles for one species of this family to nest in.
- They twitter rather than sing.

Answer: Swallows

Fish

19

What has four hearts, only one nostril, and no jaws or stomach?

Clues:

- It can live for months without feeding.
- It has "teeth" on its tongue.
- It can tie itself in a knot.
- It "sniffs" out its food.
- It has no known natural predators.
- Over a century ago, a prize was offered for the solution to the question of how it reproduces. No one has been able to claim the reward yet.
- It's sometimes called the slime eel.
- It belongs to a class of animals that includes the blood-sucking lampreys.

Answer: Hagfish

20

What animal sleeps in a "nightgown"?

Clues:

- This nightgown is a mucous sac that is secreted every night.
- The animal feeds on algae.
- It is a major source of reef erosion.
- It swallows coral as well as algae, as the algae live in the corals.
- It is gaudy-colored, has bug eyes, and a beaklike mouth.
- It belongs to the family *Scaridae*.
- One group of this animal is known as "blimpheads."

Answer: Parrot fish

Insects

21

What did Mark Twain describe as a "blundering, inept wanderer more likely to acquire some worthless article than food"?

Clues:

- No other insect or animal can trace its ancestry as far back.
- They live in a strictly ordered society based on the principle "all for one and one for all."
- The female is the longest-lived of any insect.
- There are more of these on earth than any one kind of living creature.
- If humans had the same strength ratio, they could drag a diesel railroad engine from New York to Los Angeles over mountains and plains.
- They range in size from 1/25th of an inch long to one inch long.

Answer: Ants

22

What animals do not grow in size as they become older?

Clues:

- Some varieties of this animal live near the north and south poles.
- They make up the second largest order in the animal kingdom, next to beetles.
- It begins life as an egg.
- In its adult stage it can neither bite nor chew.
- Some need to walk on their food to taste it.
- There are 700 species in North America.
- The largest have wingspreads of about five inches.
- Thistles and nettles are among their most valuable food sources.
- Some common names of these are: Dog's Head, American Tortoise, Buckeye, Cabbage, and Snout.

Answer: Butterflies

23

What eats food, garbage, clothing, furniture, and other insects?

Clues:

- It has a flattened, slippery body, covered with leathery casings.
- There are more than a thousand species.
- Strong legs permit it to run rapidly.
- It has long antennae.
- It is related to grasshoppers and crickets.
- One kind was named because it was found in the Croton waterworks system of New York City.
- It is among the oldest fossil insects.
- It is nocturnal in habit, hiding during the day.
- It is dirty and contaminates everything it touches.

Answer: Cockroach

24

What has muscles that make up a quarter of its entire weight?

Clues:

- It sheds its skin, or molts, 10-15 times.
- There are more than 2,500 known species of this, of which 300 can be found in the United States.
- It is preyed upon by hawks, swallows, frogs, watersnakes, and trout.
- As nymph, its lower lip is so large that it must be folded back under the legs.
- One was said to consume 40 horseflies in two hours.
- Upon leaving the nymphal shell, its wings must harden for several hours before it can fly.
- It is also known as Devil's Darning Needle.

Answer: Dragonfly

25

What animal has served science admirably in space experiments and other research?

Clues:

- Some species are the most dangerous of all animals.
- They breathe from the sides of their body.
- They turn solids to liquids with saliva.
- Some are so tiny they are felt rather than seen.
- They help keep the air pure by devouring carcasses.
- They see with five eyes in all directions.
- One variety travels 50 mph and another variety beats its wings 1,000 times per second.
- They breed over 18 generations in a single season.
- They can walk upside down on six legs.

Answer: Flies

26

What animal is worth millions of dollars a year to agriculture?

Clues:

- There are 4,300 known species.
- Species in the western United States fly to the mountains for the winter.
- The adults hibernate over winter.
- In the Middle Ages they were dedicated to the Virgin Mary.
- Most rise backward at first and then zoom forward.
- Their wings flutter 75-91 times a second.
- As many as 30 million may inhabit a quarter of an acre.
- Some indoor gardeners keep boxes of them in their refrigerators.

Answer: Ladybugs (also known as ladybird beetles and lady beetles)

27

What is among the deadliest enemies of humans and domestic animals?

Clues:

- None of these are native to the Hawaiian Islands, but now three different kinds live there.
- There are almost 2,000 different known kinds.
- They all begin their lives as eggs.
- Their legs have five joints and the last joint ends in a tiny pair of claws.
- In the far North, great swarms have been known to sting animals to death.
- Swarms sometimes fly into cities as far as 20 miles from where they originated.
- Diseases spread by them have been responsible for the downfall of some ancient civilizations around the Mediterranean Sea.
- Some varieties spread such deadly diseases as malaria and yellow fever.

Answer: Mosquitoes

28

What will devour its own mate, sisters, or brothers and then wash its face like a cat?

Clues:

- It can lift 24 times its own weight.
- It uses camouflage to blend in with vegetation.
- It is also called a mule killer, devil's rear horse, soothsayer, or prophet.
- It is a capable flier, and has been found on the 86th story observation level of the Empire State Building.
- It prefers to eat beetles, crickets, and other insects, but large species have been known to attack frogs, snakes, mice, and even household pets.
- It's the most voracious predator in the insect world.
- It can be a gardener's best friend.

Answer: Praying mantis

29

What walks so slowly it hardly seems alive.

Clues:

- It can eject a foul-smelling liquid.
- It has three pairs of legs.
- If caught by a leg, it can break the leg off and escape.
- Self-amputation, or autotomy, allows regeneration of parts on this animal.
- The young ones molt, or shed their skins, five or six times before becoming adults.
- It is a greedy leaf-eater and may sometimes harm trees.
- Those in the United States have no wings.
- It cannot bite, sting, or hurry.
- Camouflage is its defense.

Answer: Walking stick

Mammals

30

What animals have been mistakenly branded as grave robbers?

Clues:

- The number of teeth they have varies from several dozen up to 90, all similar and without enamel or roots.
- They gulp large quantities of air to make themselves float in water.
- In South America they range in size from five inches to a whopping 100 pounds and five feet long.
- A Mayan legend suggests that the blackheaded vulture does not die of old age, but rather sheds its wings and metamorphoses into this animal.
- Litters usually number four to eight infants of the same sex, all identical in size, soft-shelled, and with the ability to see at birth.
- They are the only known animals other than humans susceptible to leprosy.
- They are closely related to the extinct geyptodonts.
- They can be found in all southern states and as far north as Kansas.
- During the Depression they were known as "Hoover hogs."
- Their armor plate is composed of tiny checker-shaped bones fused solidly together.

Answer: Armadillos

31

What animal has a warning signal that can be heard from half a mile away?

Clues:

- When full-grown, it weighs about the same as a seven-year-old child.
- It was on earth during the Ice Age.
- The earliest ones were as large as bears.
- Its teeth are constantly growing.
- It can stay underwater for as long as 10 minutes.
- Its home is split-level with no windows.
- It belongs to the family of rodents.
- It is the greatest animal engineer.

Answer: Beaver

32

What is North America's rarest mammal?

Clues:

- It has always been very rare.
- It lives in the western United States.
- Its cousin living in Europe is trained to drive rabbits and other animals from their holes.
- It preys on prairie dogs and may use their burrows as a nest.
- It is active at dusk and at night.
- When frightened, it makes a chattering, scolding noise and hisses.
- It was first described by John J. Audubon.
- It has a tan body with feet and tail tipped black.

Answer: Black-footed ferret

33

What animal was essential to Westerners exploring and settling the New World?

Clues:

- It can scent water farther than any other animal except the camel.
- It can get by with a drink every 20-24 hours in summer—every three days in winter.
- It can stand extreme cold and searing heat.
- It has no natural enemies.
- Its average life span is 15 years—25 years in captivity.
- It never cuts itself by running into barbed wire. If it does become entangled, it will wait to be freed.
- Legend says that it was marked with a cross because it carried Mary to Bethlehem.
- It's about the size of a Shetland pony.

Answer: Burro

34

What animal yelps like a dog and emits a surprising birdlike chirp?

Clues:

- It was part of a royal sport for 3,500 years.
- It is easy to tame.
- Its great 25-foot bounds can outdistance a racehorse for brief periods.
- It has become extinct in some areas of the world and an endangered species in other parts.
- It can outrun any earthbound creature, and only three birds—the golden eagle, the peregrine falcon, and the Indian swift—are known to fly faster.
- It can reach speeds of 45 miles per hour in two seconds.
- It is capable of speeds of 70 miles per hour in pursuit of its prey.

Answer: Cheetah

35

What smooth-skinned, legless animal is thought to be descended from four-legged, hairy animals?

Clues:

- Some change their color, depending on their surroundings.
- Some have nearly lost their vision.
- Some have beaks.
- The Greeks considered them sacred to the god Apollo.
- They may weigh up to 800 pounds.
- They generally feed on fish, using their sharp teeth to catch and hold them.
- They can swim up to 25 knots.
- Famous Pelorus Jack was protected in New Zealand for his services to ships.

Answer: Dolphins

36

What odd food did the Romans feast on?

Clues:

- They have been found in fossil form dating back 30 million years.
- They are native to Europe, Asia, and Africa.
- In their deepest winter sleep, their blood temperature may fall to a fraction of a degree above freezing.
- Their diets generally consist of fruit, nuts, insects, and bird eggs.
- They sleep during the day.
- They measure 4 to 14 inches including the tail.
- They live from two to five years.
- Weasels are their enemies.
- Lewis Carroll described a humorous one that could not be kept awake at a tea party.

Answer: Dormice

37

What animal has only four teeth other than its incisors?

Clues:

- The teeth are called grinders and they last 10 years.
- After 10 years, the grinders fall out and the animal grows a new set, but it only gets six sets throughout its life.
- When it loses its last set, the animal dies because it can't eat.
- It is a wonderful swimmer.
- Its first ancestor lived in Egypt 45 million years ago.
- Its tail weighs about 22 pounds.
- It may eat about a half ton of food a day.
- The record combined weight of the two incisors of one animal was 293 pounds.

Answer: Elephant

38

What uses a unique "sixth claw" to grasp its food?

Clues:

- It spends up to 10 or 12 hours a day eating.
- The first person from outside the area to see one was a French priest in 1868.
- It is related to the raccoon.
- Adults may reach a length of six feet and weigh more than 300 pounds.
- It is called bei shung.
- It lives in western China and Tibet.
- The first specimen to be shot by a white man was collected by Theodore and Kermit Roosevelt in 1929.
- It feeds mainly on bamboo shoots.

Answer: Giant panda

39

What animals have a heart two feet long weighing 25 pounds?

Clues:

- Rock paintings in the Sahara show that they once lived in North Africa.
- They originated in Europe and Asia.
- Their sinews were used as bow strings and for the strings of musical instruments.
- During the 1800s the skin was used to make leather harnesses and whips.
- They can run 35 miles per hour for short distances.
- Baboons, zebras, and antelopes feel safe when they are nearby as lookouts.
- They fight with their necks.
- They can be up to 19 feet tall and weigh 2,600 pounds.

Answer: Giraffes

40

What animal runs on its fingernails?

Clues:

- It never eats meat.
- It has the same number of bones in its neck as humans—seven.
- Brazil raises more of these than any other country.
- There were none found in the United States by the first European colonists.
- It has the largest eyes of any land mammals.
- Its earliest ancestor was believed to be 10-20 inches high.
- It has only one toe (or finger) on each foot.

Answer: Horse

41

What animal has underwater eyesight equal to a cat's vision?

Clues:

- It snores while sleeping.
- Its sounds have been recorded and studied.
- It has 40-48 teeth.
- It is found in all oceans.
- It can torpedo its 15-39 foot body through the water at speeds of up to 35 knots.
- It may eat its cousin, the bottlenose dolphin.
- The first one taken into captivity sold for $8,000.

Answer: Killer whale

42

What land animal can spend its entire life without stepping on land?

Clues:

- It is mainly carnivorous.
- It has little social life and seldom fights or travels with company.
- Its front paws, webbed half the length of its toes, can propel it through 100 yards of water in 33 seconds.
- A mature adult consumes between 15 and 50 pounds of meat in one meal.
- It is among the largest of its kind.
- It mates in March and April.
- Its life span may be as long as 34 years.
- Its worst enemies are humans and the walrus.
- It is said that while stalking seals over sea ice, it hides its black nose with one paw.

Answer: Polar bear

43

What animal's New World variety is arboreal, while those in the Old World are terrestrial?

Clues:

- They are nearsighted.
- They have large brains and appear to have good memories.
- They usually give birth to one offspring at a time.
- The young are born with their eyes open and able to walk.
- Their flesh is edible, but few consider it appetizing.
- Their food includes tree bark.
- They defend themselves by striking attackers with their tails.
- They have long soft hairs and strong, stiff quills on their backs, sides, and tails.

Answer: Porcupines

44

What is the fastest mammal in the Western Hemisphere?

Clues:

- It has telescopic eyes.
- It runs with its mouth open, sucking in great quantities of air through a windpipe that is twice the diameter of a human's.
- Its speed is second only to the cheetah's among all ground animals.
- It is a poor jumper.
- Woven or net wire fences are among its worst enemies.
- It has no dewclaws.
- Within a week after birth, its young can outdistance any man and most dogs.
- When it senses danger, this animal bristles the hairs of its rump to warn the others.
- It is mistakenly called "antelope."

Answer: Pronghorn

45

What animal has a howl that is so ventriloquial in effect that it sounds like a chorus?

Clues:

- It feeds primarily on small mammals, birds, and crabs.
- Its range once extended from Texas to Florida.
- Now there are fewer than 100 living in the area around the Texas-Louisiana border.
- There are no recorded cases of this animal killing a human being.
- It's on the U.S. Fish and Wildlife Services' list of rare and endangered species.
- Its species is *Canus niger rufus*.
- His cousin appears in many fairy tales.

Answer: Red wolf

46

What animal's ankles make audible clicking and snapping sounds when it moves?

Clues:

- They are fast swimmers.
- They can travel at a top speed of 32 miles per hour on land.
- Their coat is made of long cellular hair.
- They have a hairy muzzle.
- They were probably one of the prime foods of Paleolithic man.
- They are depended upon for milk, meat, fur, leather, and transportation by some people.
- Antler size is correlated with rank.
- They are hitched as many as 9 or 10 in single file to a sled.
- It is the only deer species in which both sexes have antlers.

Answer: Reindeer

47

What is considered by many to be the fiercest animal on earth?

Clues:

- It is so savage it will attack, kill, and devour animals twice its size.
- It can eat the equivalent of its own weight about every three hours.
- It burns energy so fast that if deprived of food, it will starve to death in less than a day.
- One species has salivary glands that contain a venom similar to that secreted by such poisonous snakes as the cobra.
- It can be found in most parts of the world—in the tropics, deserts, and Arctic.
- Its natural enemies (great horned owl, weasels, and bobcats) must have strong stomachs as the animals' flanks have a potent gland containing a sickening musk.
- It is best known for its pointed snout.

Answer: Shrew

48

What animal's blood was it once thought one should sip to be restored to health after being struck by lightning?

Clues:

- In ancient times, only the royal family wore cloth from its fleece and violators were killed.
- A male, with his harem, marks his territory with dung heaps.
- Shorn once a year, its yield is only 1/4 to 1/2 pound of wool.
- The gestation period is 11 months.
- A baby can outrun a man minutes after birth.
- Most young are born between 8:00 and 10:30 in the morning to avoid being rained on in the afternoon and chilled by the cold night.
- The stomach of the young, called a cria, is used to curdle milk to make cheese.
- It is a relative of the camel.

Answer: Vicuña

49

What animal lives nowhere else in the United States but Alaska?

Clues:

- It never ranges south of the ice fields.
- Although its ears are covered with muscle and skin, it can hear.
- The babies live on mother's milk for two years.
- They have relatively little hair.
- Tough bristles on its upper lip are used to strain food.
- A full-grown male may outweigh 15 men.
- It was hunted in the 1800s for lamp oil obtained from its "blanket of blubber."
- It may measure 12 feet in length.
- The polar bear is its chief enemy.
- The hides are used for roofs, boat coverings, and harnesses.
- Its tusks may be three feet long.

Answer: Walrus

50

What animal has been so inbred that today the entire species is made up of "identical twins"?

Clues:

- This animal ages at a rate 30 times faster than humans, so it is rare to find one three years old.
- Newborn babies double their weight in six days.
- It seems to have a built-in timepiece, because all mothers feed their young at the same time.
- It is highly susceptible to vitamin deficiencies.
- Beet sugar or cottonseeds can produce sterility in this animal.
- Its teeth grow constantly, and it must chew and gnaw to keep them worn down.
- Scientists like them because they cost little, eat almost anything, and are a convenient size for handling.

Answer: White rat

51

What animal's combination of bodily strength, amazing courage, and perseverance is matched by no other four-footed creature on earth?

Clues:

- It is feared by almost all other creatures in its domain, including predators much larger than it.
- It is able to climb trees.
- Its eyesight is so poor that an intruder can approach to within 50 yards before this animal sees it.
- Ernest Thompson Seton, the naturalist, gives accounts of this animal handling rocks and logs so heavy that a human would have difficulty moving them.
- It lives predominantly in Alaska and Canada, although a related species is native to northern Europe and Asia.
- Its fur, which sheds moisture, is valued for collars and parkas because it doesn't frost from the wearer's breath.
- It is rare today because it has been hunted ruthlessly.
- It is the largest member of the weasel family.

Answer: Wolverine

Marsupials

52

What animal has one species that can live in trees and leap 50 feet to the ground?

Clues:

- Most species have large, upright ears and a long muzzle like a deer.
- It seldom drinks, but gets the moisture it needs from the vegetation it eats.
- Each hind foot has four toes and is armed with one claw that is especially long and dangerous.
- It ranges in length from 16 inches to eight feet.
- It is less than an inch long at birth.
- It eats chiefly herbs and grasses.
- They are hunted for food and their hides.
- It is the largest animal that carries its young in a pouch in its abdomen.

Answer: Kangaroo

53

What is arguably the ugliest animal in the world?

Clues:

- Its legs seem too short to support its body.
- It has 42 large teeth (a cat has 30).
- It is ordinarily a scavenger, but hunts occasionally.
- Males are three feet long and weigh 20-25 pounds.
- Most of them are nocturnal.
- Stockmen say it will competely consume a dead cow or sheep—eating bones, skin, hoofs, horns, and hair.
- It is covered with jet-black hair usually splashed with white blazes across chest and rump.
- Its ears are batlike; its nose is piggish, and it has long, coarse whiskers.
- When born, it is about the size of a honeybee. It crawls through its mother's fur to her pouch and affixes itself to teats where it remains for several months.
- It lives in the southernmost state of Australia.

Answer: Tasmanian devil

Reptiles

54

What animal carries its food reserves in its tail?

Clues:

- It samples ground odors with its tongue.
- It has powerful jaws that can be opened only with force.
- Its eggs are the size of hen's eggs.
- It eats bird and reptile eggs and small animals.
- Poison formed in modified salivary glands runs down grooves in the lower teeth and is worked into a wound by jaw action.
- Its beaded skin makes it easily identified. Each bead-like bump contains a small bony core.
- One species was first found near the Gila River in Arizona.

Answer: Gila monster

55

What animal has no ears?

Clues:

- It breathes by a lung.
- Some can digest bones.
- Some have more than 300 pairs of ribs.
- The teeth all curve inward.
- It never stops growing as long as it lives.
- Some are hatched from eggs and others are born live.
- It sleeps with its eyes open.
- It grows a complete new skin several times a year.
- It is covered with convex overlapping scales from the tip of the nose to the tip of the tail.

Answer: Snake

56

What animal's eggs take from 13-15 months to hatch?

Clues:

- It takes the animal about 30 years to reach its full growth.
- It is a living fossil.
- The male is 60 centimeters long when full grown.
- It eats very little—seldom more than a few insects a day.
- It is most active at temperatures around 12 degrees C.
- Its name means "peaks on the back."
- It can be found only on a few of New Zealand's smallest islands.
- It is not a lizard.
- It is the only remaining species of the order Rhynchocephalia.

Answer: Tuatara

Plants

Fungi

57

What domesticated life form have humans been using in food preparation since 2,000 B.C.?

Clues:

- They feed on dead plant materials.
- Some cause skin infections.
- They can be rich in minerals, proteins, carbohydrates, and vitamin B.
- Of our domestic variety, one unit is 1/3,000-inch wide.
- They cannot manufacture their own foods from minerals in the soil.
- They have no chlorophyll.
- Reproduction is by budding.
- They require dissolved sugar for food.
- They can stand dryness and cold, but are killed by heat near 212 degrees F.

Answer: Yeasts

Grasses

58

What plant has the tensile strength of iron?

Clues:

- This product is more profitable than iron.
- It is able to survive typhoons and even survived the atomic bombing of Hiroshima, Japan.
- When it flowers, it dies.
- It grows faster than anything else on earth.
- It is considered a weed in Hawaii and cracks roads, runways, and walls.
- It isn't a tree but a grass.
- In more than 2,000 years, it has been painted more often, and with more devotion, than any living thing other than human beings.
- Rhizome and culm serve as root and trunk.

Answer: Bamboo

Cultivated Plants

59

What plant did the Egyptians grow in the early days of the pharoahs, believing that good luck would bless those who ate it?

Clues:

- The plant is native to South America.
- It is not recommended for soups because of its strong flavor.
- The dry seed is very high in protein, fat, and carbohydrates.
- Athens, Texas, is the world capital of this plant.
- It is a legume.
- Both canned and dried varieties are shipped all over the world and can be found in most stores.
- One of its names is similar to an animal we all know.

Answer: Black-eyed pea or cowpea

60

What was thought to be the first lightning rod?

Clues:

- Greeks grew them around their homes as protection from lightning.
- Its fresh leaves strewn on floors can drive away fleas.
- It is one of the most common wild plants in the world.
- Botanists know it as a wild chrysanthemum.
- One popular cultivated variety was developed by Luther Burbank.
- It is known in Europe as the marguerite.
- Farmers called it whiteweed.
- Its name comes from the Old English words, "day's eye," which refer to the fact that its blossoms open at dawn and close at night.

Answer: Daisy

61

What herb is a potent antiseptic?

Clues:

- Workers building the Great Pyramid reportedly went on strike when supplies ran short.
- It was cultivated in Egypt at least 4,800 years ago.
- It is sometimes applied to skin to alleviate the pain of insect or scorpion stings.
- The Indian name for it was the basis for the name of Chicago. It used to grow wild where the city stands today.
- Some health food enthusiasts believe a cold can be cured by rubbing it on the soles of the feet.
- Botanists consider it a member of either the amaryllis or lily family.
- It has long been indispensable in cooking in France, Spain, Italy, Greece, and elsewhere around the Mediterranean.

Answer: Garlic

62

The medieval "soporific sponge" that would knock out a grown man if he took one whiff was soaked in mandrake, hemlock, poppy, ivy, mulberry, and what?

Clues:

- The wild variety was brewed into a tea by the Meskwakie Indians and given to women following childbirth to increase the new mothers' milk.
- White settlers used the wild variety to make a sedative syrup for babies.
- It probably originated in southern Europe or western Asia.
- It is grown from seed and has been cultivated for 2,500 years.
- High temperatures lead to inferior quality.
- It is rich in vitamin A and is low in calories.
- It is cultivated in 20 states, with California the leading producer.
- The three main kinds are cos, leaf, and head, and there are also wild and celtuce varieties.

Answer: Lettuce

63

What plant has registration of hybrids, judging, and awards similar to the system used by dog and cattle breeders?

Clues:

- They grow from the Arctic Circle to the tropics.
- Two Australian species are subterranean, growing and flowering underground.
- This is probably the largest plant family, exceeding even the daisy family.
- The seeds are so small, they look almost like powder.
- To grow, the seeds form a relationship with microscopic fungi, which provide them with food.
- Vanilla flavoring is obtained from the seed pods of one species.
- The best known and most widely used variety is the Cattleya.

Answer: Orchids

64

What plant was worn around the neck in ancient times in the belief it could prevent intoxication?

Clues:

- It was first grown in Sardinia and southern Italy.
- In Medieval Europe, black magic ritual prescribed it to do away with one's enemies.
- An old country belief in England held that only the wicked could grow it.
- The roots of one variety are eaten as a vegetable in Europe.
- The Greeks used it to crown victors at the Isthmian games.
- It is high in vitamins A and C and in iron.
- It is grown in California in great quantities to be dehydrated.
- It is one of the commonest plants used in garnishing fish and meats.

Answer: Parsley

65

What plant, for a century after its discovery, was said to cause leprosy, tuberculosis, and rickets?

Clues:

- Queen Marie Antoinette wore its blossoms in her hair at a reception.
- Benjamin Franklin ate it at a dinner in France in which the whole menu consisted of the plant's fruit cooked in various ways.
- Russia grows about 33 percent of the world's production.
- Its fruits are a good source of low-cost vitamins and minerals.
- It's grown in every state in the United States.
- It was eaten by the Incas and was then small and yellow-fleshed.
- From 1845-1847, about 750,000 people died in Ireland because of crop failure of this plant.

Answer: Potato

66

What is eaten by people, cats, and dogs, yet is in the paint of your walls, in insecticides, and in antibiotics?

Clues:

- It is also found in disinfectants, linoleum backing, birth control pills, liquid makeup, ink, and marshmallows.
- It is used extensively in research of the brain.
- It was native to the Far East where it has been cultivated for probably 5,000 years.
- It didn't come to the U.S. until early this century.
- Prior to 1940, the fruit was used as fertilizer.
- You can buy them raw, cooked, canned, and roasted.
- Only 3 percent of an annual world yield of two billion bushels ever reaches U.S. tabletops.

Answer: Soybean (or soya bean)

67

Speculation in what commodity brought a nation to the brink of financial ruin between 1634 and 1637?

Clues:

- It was brought from Turkey in the sixteenth century.
- It exudes small amounts of ethylene gas.
- Its head is fed to cows.
- The largest auction house in the world, where it is sold, covers an area equal to 30 football fields.
- New hybrids can reach 36″ in height.
- It can be grown from seed, but it takes so long that most people grow it only from bulbs.
- It belongs to the lily family.
- The name comes from a Turkish word for "turban."
- It is a major industry in Holland.

Answer: Tulip

Parasitic Plants

68

What was regarded as sacred by the ancient Druids and was worn as a charm?

Clues:

- It has tiny yellow flowers that bloom in February and March.
- It is propagated from tree to tree by sticky white berries that cling to the birds that feed on them.
- The berries may be poisonous to people.
- Balder, son of the Norse goddess, Frigg, was said to have been killed by an arrow made of it.
- It is an evergreen and a parasite.
- It is the state flower of Oklahoma.
- When passing under it, people of opposite sexes give each other the kiss of peace and love to prove it no longer is an instrument of mischief.

Answer: Mistletoe

Wild Plants

69

What came to America with the early colonists and subsequently conquered it?

Clues:

- It is native to Europe and Asia.
- The people on the island of Majorca survived by eating this after all other vegetation was destroyed by a grasshopper plague.
- Our ancestors cooked its roots like carrots.
- Its blossom is actually a bouquet of 150-200 tiny flowers.
- Vineland, New Jersey, is the world capital of this plant.
- It adapts to any temperate climate and thrives in almost any soil.
- Its roots can grow to five feet in length.
- There are recipes for using it in foods from wine to gelatin.
- Its name is derived from the French word meaning "lion's tooth."

Answer: Dandelion

70

What demonstrates nature's abhorrence of ugliness by beautifying landscapes devasted by the woodsman's axe and forest fire?

Clues:

- It is common throughout Europe, Asia, and North America.
- It ranges in height from two to eight feet.
- Flower colors range from purple-lavender, through magenta and pink, to an occasional white.
- Beginning at the bottom of the long spike, the flowers open in slow succession upward throughout summer into the fall.
- The seeds, tufted with white hairs, make the plant look shaggy in the fall.
- It is in the evening primrose family.
- It is also called great willow herb or wickup.
- It is the official flower of the Yukon Territory.

Answer: Fireweed

71

What source of natural rubber is not economically feasible to use?

Clues:

- The leaves produce an oil used as a tonic.
- The leaves of one variety are used to make tea.
- Thomas A. Edison has one kind named for him.
- They are tenderly cultivated in gardens in Europe.
- Most of the more than 100 species are native to North America.
- Some normally grow to about 10 feet.
- It is the state flower of more than one state.
- It is erroneously blamed for hayfever usually caused by ragweed.

Answer: Goldenrod

72

Which plant can change sex?

Clues:

- The plant isn't fixed as male or female, but has the option each year of performing as either sex.
- The plant is poisonous when eaten raw.
- The juice of the root is sometimes used in homemade cough medicine.
- It thrives in moist woods.
- Only snails and slugs feed on its foliage with any regularity.
- Large (knee-high) plants may be 20 or more years old.
- It develops only one or two leaves.
- It is also called Indian turnip.

Answer: Jack-in-the-pulpit

73

What covers about a million acres of southern fields?

Clues:

- In 1876, Japan displayed this at the U.S. Centennial Celebration.
- The weight of it can break telephone lines and it can grow a foot a day.
- In Japan, the people use its starchy roots for food and feed the leaves to their livestock.
- It has natural enemies in the Far East.
- It does best with long growing seasons and plenty of water.
- It covers trees and kills forests by cutting out the light source.
- At first Americans liked it because it slowed soil erosion, held roadbanks in place, and helped enrich the soil, but now scientists hope to find a way to wipe it out.
- The vines grow so fast some people call it "the mile-a-minute plant."

Answer: Kudzu

74

What species is really made up of a partnership between two organisms, but is given a single genus and species name?

Clues:

- The slower growing ones may be 4,000 years old.
- Harris-tweed fabrics get their color from this species.
- The Biblical manna is thought by many to be this species.
- Varieties are used in the manufacture of perfumes and antibiotics.
- Varieties grow in higher elevations and nearer to the poles than any other plants, but also flourish near the equator.
- They are used in salves that heal burns and wounds better than penicillin.
- They can survive colds of -27.3 degrees C and heat twice that of boiling water (434 degrees F).
- Pollution is killing them off.
- Laplanders dry them for fodder.
- They help break rocks into particles to form soil.

Answer: Lichens

75

What plant generates its own heat and maintains a nearly constant temperature of 72 degrees?

Clues:

- Some may exceed the age of oaks.
- Indians and pioneers used it for treatment of headache, asthma, bruises, toothache, and to stop bleeding.
- It contains calcium oxalate.
- It is often found in a small puddle of water surrounded by frozen earth.
- It belongs to the Arum family.
- It has a fetid odor.

Answer: Skunk cabbage

76

What, according to Charles Darwin, is the "most wonderful plant in the world"?

Clues:

- It grows about a foot high.
- It was discovered by Arthur Dobbs, governor of North Carolina, and reported in a letter dated January 24, 1760.
- It was once thought to have been left behind after a visit from outer space.
- Its nectar may be able to be used to develop a biological insect control,
- Its green jaws stand ajar like an empty clamshell.
- Once it finds something to eat, it requires about 10 days to digest its food.
- It lives in sandy soil that lacks nitrogen that the plant needs. It gets its nitrogen from insect protein.

Answer: Venus flytrap

Shrubs

77

What plant grows mostly in eastern North America and China?

Clues:

- In some varieties, the flower has a covering of sticky hairs that keeps ants away from the nectar.
- About 40 species grow in North America.
- They live best in acid soil and in partial shade.
- They bloom early in May and June.
- They range in color through all shades of purple, red, white, yellow, and pink.
- They may bloom before their leaves open.
- They grow in gardens and wild in woods and swampy areas.
- Botanists classify them as being of the genus Rhododendron.

Answer: Azalea

Trees

78

What is the most widely distributed tree species in North America?

Clues:

- It grows from coast to coast in the United States and Canada and north to Alaska.
- Indians and early settlers claimed that tea made from its bark could cure fevers, colds, and constipation.
- According to the legends of the French-Canadian trappers, Christ's cross was made of this wood.
- Lumbermen regard it as a "weed" tree.
- It was used as cattle feed during the Great Depression.
- Most of its wood goes into pulp that makes magazine and book paper.
- It is the first tree to grow after a forest fire.
- Its saw-toothed leaves are shiny green on top and silvery green beneath.

Answer: Aspen

79

What plant has an edible growth that keeps almost forever when dried.

Clues:

- Its hearts are a well-known delicacy.
- It needs to be pollinated by hand as its main growing area doesn't have a wide variety of insect species.
- Its seeds can lie dormant for years before germinating when conditions are favorable.
- It has been eaten by humans for 7,000-8,000 years.
- It is cultivated on a limited but productive scale in southern California.
- It has a sugar content so high (80 percent) that it inhibits most germs and so provides a healthy food for the tropics.
- It is unlawful for Muslims to drink its juice if it ferments more than three days.
- Pressed into cakes, it is used to feed camels, horses, and even dogs when little else is available.
- It is in the center of the royal emblem of Saudi Arabia.

Answer: Date palm

80

What plant is as hard as a rock?

Clues:

- English physicians considered the fruit a cure for colic, but this sometimes proved fatal.
- Tea made from its leaves is harmless to drink.
- The Midwest's largest producer of this is Indiana.
- Folklore suggests that George Washington's false teeth were made from this material, but in fact they were made of ivory and wooden pegs.
- The bark is used to make birdlime in some countries for entangling small birds.
- It is used for musical instruments, furniture, and interior decoration.
- Legend says that the berries were white until the Christ child pricked his finger on the leaves. The plant blushed red in shame.
- It is known as the holy tree.

Answer: Holly

People

Abolitionists

81

Who was attached to the Union Army in South Carolina and served as a cook, nurse, and scout for raiding parties?

Clues:

- This person acted as a spy behind Confederate lines.
- Rewards for the capture of this person once totaled $40,000.
- When she was 13, an enraged supervisor fractured her skull with a two-pound weight.
- Her father taught her a knowledge of the woods.
- She never learned to read or write.
- Citizens of Auburn, New York, raised a monument to her memory.
- A U.S. postage stamp bearing her portrait was issued in 1978.
- She helped more than 300 slaves escape to freedom.
- Her efforts to free slaves earned her the name "Moses."

Answer: Harriet Tubman

American Presidents and First Families

82

Who began his business career selling on the streets at the age of five?

Clues:

- He was an electronics instructor.
- His favorite sport is stock car racing.
- He served as chairman on his local County Board of Education.
- He studied modern farming techniques at the Agricultural Experiment Station.
- He was the engineering officer of a nuclear submarine.
- He has been nominated for the Nobel Peace prize several times for his diplomatic efforts.
- He was not re-elected to office.
- He was the first president of the United States to be elected from the "deep South" since before the Civil War.

Answer: Jimmy Carter

83

Who had the Russian Order of Victory bestowed upon him (a decoration awarded to only seven other men and never before a non-Russian)?

Clues:

- At one time he worked in a dairy, 84 hours a week.
- He played football against Jim Thorpe.
- Although threatened with death from blood poisoning, he refused to allow the amputation of his leg.
- He said, "Only strength can cooperate. Weakness cannot cooperate. It can only beg."
- He gained recognition as a planner and strategist.
- Twice he refused to run for the presidency.
- He became president of Columbia University.
- He was Supreme Allied Commander in World War II.
- He was the 34th president of the United States.

Answer: Dwight D. Eisenhower

84

Who proposed the decimal monetary system for the United States?

Clues:

- As a scientific farmer, he cultivated the finest gardens in America.
- He was the foremost architect of his time.
- He invented the swivel chair and the dumbwaiter.
- He founded Virginia's state university.
- He prepared written vocabularies of some Native American languages.
- His personal library became the nucleus of the Library of Congress.
- He founded the Democratic party.
- He wrote the Declaration of Independence.

Answer: Thomas Jefferson

85

Who was the only southerner to remain in the Senate when the Civil War broke out?

Clues:

- He went to work at age 10.
- He taught himself to read.
- He was employed as a tailor.
- He became well known as a strong supporter of a generous homestead law.
- He was appointed military governor of Tennessee.
- He issued a proclamation pardoning most southerners charged with criminal rebellion if they took an oath of allegiance to the United States.
- He was the only president who never went to school.
- He was the 17th president of the United States.

Answer: Andrew Johnson

86

Who was known at one time as the "unofficial first lady"?

Clues:

- Without her intercession it is possible that "The Star Spangled Banner" would never have been written.
- She started the annual egg-roll on the White House lawn on Easter Monday.
- She slept with a Tunisian saber (a souvenir of the war with the Barbary pirates) beside her bed.
- She was expelled from the Society of Friends, or Quakers.
- She was criticized for using snuff in public.
- Aaron Burr was among her suitors.
- She was voted a seat on the floor of the House of Representatives.
- She managed to save many of the nation's valuable papers and a portrait before her home was burned.

Answer: Dolley Madison (also spelled Dolly)

87

Who, at age 18, led his men in Washington's crossing of the Delaware on Christmas night?

Clues:

- A bullet he received at Trenton remained in his shoulder for the rest of his life.
- He was an ardent supporter of the French Revolution.
- He was elected governor of Virginia twice.
- He secured peaceful boundaries with Canada.
- The capital of the first Negro republic, Liberia, was named after him.
- He was re-elected to the presidency by the amazing electoral vote of 231 to 1.
- He considered the negotiation with Napoleon for the sale of the Louisiana Territory his most important public service.

Answer: James Monroe

88

Who, although a slave owner himself, urged admission of California, a free state, to the Union?

Clues:

- Rumor had it that his wife smoked a corncob pipe in the privacy of her room.
- He grew up on "the dark and bloody ground" of Kentucky's frontier.
- He never lost a battle.
- He won a stunning victory at the Battle of Buena Vista.
- He defeated the Seminole Indians at Lake Okeechobee.
- His son-in-law was president of the Confederacy.
- His troops called him "Old Rough and Ready."
- Although he would normally have taken office on March 4, he declined to be inaugurated as president on a Sunday.

Answer: Zachary Taylor

89

Who is believed by some to have died due to bloodletting?

Clues:

- After he caught a cold, his doctors were overenthusiastic about drawing blood from his body. They weakened him until he died.
- He could fell a tree like a lumberjack.
- He could work iron like a blacksmith.
- His first big job was to survey the estate of his neighbor whose royal grant of six million acres ran from the Atlantic seaboard to the Alleghenies.
- Carrying a message to the French officer at Fort LeBoeuf, he crossed the Alleghenies in the dress of an Indian scout.
- He stood over 6′ 4″ and wore a size 13 shoe.
- In one battle he had two horses shot from under him and four bullets passed through his coat.
- Some men tried to crown him King of America.

Answer: George Washington

Artists

90

Who attempted to sell a piece of sculpture as an antiquity by burying it in the ground?

Clues:

- He spent months illegally dissecting corpses.
- While young he got into a fight that disfigured him for life.
- When he died, his body was spirited away from Rome disguised as mercantile goods.
- He painted an area that covered more than 10,000 square feet.
- He was sculptor, artist, architect, and poet.
- The structure and decoration of St. Peter's Basilica, except for the facade and first two bays, are indelibly his work.
- The dome he engineered influenced many buildings, including the Capitol in Washington, D.C.
- One of his works was the Vatican's main attraction at the 1964 New York World's Fair.

Answer: Michelangelo

Athletes

91

Who was originally "discovered" on a kindergarten playground?

Clues:

- Her training included running, pushups, and situps.
- She finished in 13th place in her first competition.
- Her favorite part of America is Disneyland.
- She made the covers of *Time*, *Newsweek*, and *Sports Illustrated* all in one week, the first time in the history of the magazines that one person was on all three covers at the same time.
- She became the first gymnast in the history of the modern Olympic Games to score a perfect 10.
- Sportswriters called her the "child heroine" of the XXI Olympiad.
- She was born in Romania.

Answer: Nadia Comaneci

92

Who became a leading box-office attraction in the motion-picture industry based on athletic talent?

Clues:

- At five, this person won a 40-meter footrace in Denmark.
- At seven, this person won a junior skiing competition.
- She was known as "the wonder child."
- At age 12 she was asked to represent her country in the Olympics.
- No female athlete in history has ever been a champion in Olympic competition for as many years.
- She won the gold medal in the Olympics three times in a row before she retired from amateur competition.
- When she was only nine, she won the women's figure skating championship for the city of Oslo.
- She was called the "girl in white" and the "Norwegian doll."
- She became a naturalized United States citizen in 1941.

Answer: Sonja Henie

93

Which professional athlete was cut from his high school team as a sophomore?

Clues:

- He was short and underweight at 14.
- He is an excellent golfer.
- By his senior year he was 6′ 6½″ tall.
- He spent summers working with young people at sports camps.
- He was named Rookie of the Year.
- He racked up 59 points during 37 minutes of play in one game.
- His father was murdered.
- He played with the Dream Team in the 1992 Olympics at Barcelona, Spain.
- He retired in 1993.

Answer: Michael Jordan

94

Who was known as the "Great Black Hope"?

Clues:

- He is known by only his first and middle names, not his last name.
- He grossed four million dollars in his career.
- One of his opponents screamed so loudly (from a fractured rib being driven against his kidney) that the scream was heard many rows from ringside above the roar of the 70,000 spectators.
- He was a Golden Glove winner.
- In his career he lost only one decision.
- He defended his title more than any man in the history of boxing.
- He held the world's heavyweight championship for 12 straight years.

Answer: Joe Louis

95

Who described himself as an "American Airedale of sorts"?

Clues:

- At age 15 he weighed 115 pounds.
- His great-grandfather was Chief Black Hawk, the last and finest warrior of the Sac and Fox tribes of the Algonquian language group.
- He was known as Wa-Tho-Huck, which means "Bright Path."
- Dwight D. Eisenhower played right halfback for Army against him and never was hit so hard nor hurt so much.
- In a track meet with Lafayette College, he took first in high jump, pole vault, shot put, and low hurdles.
- He was a star passer, punter, and dropkicker and was a master at blocking and end running.
- A king once called him the world's greatest all-around athlete.
- He was the first president of the American Professional Football League.

Answer: Jim Thorpe

Authors

96

Who arrived with a comet and departed with a comet?

Clues:

- He attended school in a small log cabin.
- His mother sewed his shirt at the collar so that she could tell whether he had played hooky to go swimming.
- After he nearly drowned, his mother said, "I guess he wasn't in too much danger. People born to be hanged are safe in water."
- He enlisted in the Confederate Army but managed to get himself discharged after two weeks.
- He tried prospecting in Carson City, Nevada.
- His pen name was first used by Captain Isaiah Sellers, a writer for the *New Orleans Picayune*.
- Upon hearing a rumor that he was dead, he remarked, "The rumors of my death are greatly exaggerated."
- His pseudonym means "two fathoms deep and safe water."

Answer: Samuel Langhorne Clemens (Mark Twain)

Aviators

97

Who was the racing pilot who was victorious in the Schneider Cup, Bendix Trophy, and Thompson Trophy?

Clues:

- At 15 he was the amateur flyweight boxing champion of the Pacific coast.
- He lived in Nome, Alaska, for eight years.
- He wrote his theses for his master's and doctor's degrees on precise effects of gravity on the body and about the wind-gradient factor.
- He was the first pilot credited with an outside loop.
- He made history's first blind takeoff and landing.
- He was the first pilot to fly across the continent in less than 24 hours.
- He promoted the production and use of 100-octane fuel.
- April 18, 1942, he led a flight of B-25 bombers on a successful strike on Tokyo.

Answer: James H. ("General Jimmy") Doolittle

Entertainers

98

Who thrilled the world as Agathe, Amina, Alice, Martha, Susanna, Norma, and Lucia?

Clues:

- At the age of 21 she was told her career was over.
- The *Ugly Duckling* was written about her.
- She fell in love with Felix Mendelssohn but married Otto Goldschmidt.
- In 1850, she was the most popular woman in the world based on news articles and ticket sales.
- She received a watch from the Queen of Sweden, a golden shoe from the King of Denmark, and a jeweled nightingale from the Queen of England.
- She toured in the United States for P. T. Barnum.
- She was known as the "Swedish Nightingale."

Answer: Jenny Lind

99

Which famous personality's grandfather was a Nobel Prize Winner?

Clues:

- At one time she wanted to become a veterinarian.
- She spends more money on her animals than on herself.
- One parent was a college German professor.
- She sang at the Metropolitan Opera.
- She won a Haley Mills look-alike contest.
- She sang in a group called Sol 4.
- Her first record turned into a hit single.
- She won a Grammy for best country performance by a female star in 1974.

Answer: Olivia Newton-John

100

Who was said to be "unspeakably untalented" and "a voodoo of frustration and defiance"?

Clues:

- He played end on his high school football team.
- His parents were too poor to afford a telephone.
- Two people were killed while mourning him.
- He often wore pink and black.
- One talent agent said he should think about going back to driving a truck.
- The Mississippi State Legislature passed a resolution stating that he had become a legend and an inspiration to tens of millions of Americans.
- His song, "Hound Dog," was world famous.

Answer: Elvis Presley

101

Who was described as "a real person in the fake world of TV" by *Newsday* columnist Marvin Kitman?

Clues:

- Her first name was changed when the midwife accidentally transposed the second and third letters on her birth certificate.
- She was born in Mississippi.
- Having learned to read at age 2½, she wrote a note to her kindergarten teacher pointing out that she should be in first grade and was promptly promoted.
- At 12 she earned $500 for a speech she delivered at a church.
- She narrated a highly praised program focusing on child abuse within families.
- She became the first black woman to serve as coanchor on the Nashville evening news.
- She became producer and host of ABC's "Afterschool Specials."
- Her talk show overtook Phil Donahue's in Chicago.

Answer: Oprah Winfrey

Explorers

102

Who was kidnapped and sold to a Frenchman at an early age?

Clues:

- This person adopted a dead sister's child and according to custom never admitted that the child was someone else's.
- A river, a peak, and a mountain pass are named for this person.
- With her baby strapped to her back, she rescued important records from an overturned canoe.
- She was administered a small portion of the rattle of a rattlesnake when giving birth to her son.
- She had more than one name, but one meant "Grass Maiden."
- A shrewd sense and good counsel prevailed over a brother's determination to destroy the whites for their goods.
- She knew the Yellowstone region well.
- William Clark nicknamed her Janey.

Answer: Sacajawea

Inventors

103

Who stuffed paper into his telephone bell to prevent it from interrupting his work?

Clues:

- He perfected a hydroplane.
- For 30 years, he directed breeding experiments in an attempt to develop a strain of sheep that would bear more than one lamb at a time.
- He developed an electrical apparatus to locate bullets and other metal in the body in a vain effort to save President James Garfield's life.
- In 1912, he put forth a plea for World English, a universal language based on phonetics of the English language.
- He wanted to be remembered as a teacher of the deaf.
- His most famous words were, "Mr. Watson, come here, please. I want you."

Answer: Alexander Graham Bell

104

Who printed the first newspaper to be published on a moving train?

Clues:

- He offered a program for farm relief.
- As a child his curiosity led him to put hen and goose eggs in a basket and try to hatch them by sitting on them.
- He predicted the use of atomic energy.
- He had only three months of formal schooling.
- He did not mind being deaf because it made it easier to concentrate.
- He defined genius as 1 percent inspiration and 99 percent perspiration.
- He patented 1,093 inventions in his lifetime.

Answer: Thomas A. Edison

Journalists

105

Who was the first person to surpass the feat of the fictional hero of Jules Verne's novel *Around the World in 80 Days*?

Clues:

- The trip took 72 days, six hours and 11 minutes.
- She was born in 1867.
- She was an American journalist.
- In 1887, she traveled through Mexico sending back travel reports to her paper.
- She had herself committed to an insane asylum and then wrote a series of stories *Ten Days in a Madhouse*. Her book caused a grand jury investigation of the asylum and brought about some improvements in patient care.
- After her husband's death, she attended to his business interests, the manufacture of iron and steel.
- Her pen name was taken from a song by Stephen Foster.

Answer: Elizabeth Cochran Seamen (Nellie Bly)

Jurists

106

Who conducted himself honorably when the French tried to bribe members of a U.S. diplomatic mission sent to negotiate the matter of French interference in American trade?

Clues:

- He was a backwoodsman from Virginia.
- He was at Valley Forge during the winter of 1777-1778.
- He said he had gone into the army a Virginian and came out an American.
- He was often threatened with impeachment by those who opposed him.
- At one time he was a congressman.
- It was his conduct in the notorious XYZ Affair that made him a popular national figure.
- The Liberty Bell cracked while being rung in mourning of his death.
- Recent court interpretations have rested heavily upon his strong principles.
- He was Chief Justice of the Supreme Court from 1801-1835.

Answer: John Marshall

Military Leaders

107

Who was laid to rest in the cathedral where Poland's kings are buried while his heart is in the Polish Museum in Switzerland?

Clues:

- Thomas Jefferson provided him with false passports.
- He became an aide of George Washington.
- He refused the promotion George Washington gave him.
- He was the engineer who planned the battle site at Saratoga.
- In payment for his help in the Revolution, Congress gave him a grant of 500 acres located near what is now Columbus, Ohio.
- In 1793, he lead an army in his home country against the Russians who occupied it.
- He wrote a paper on "Manoeuvers for Horse Artillery" which was adopted for use by the U.S. during the War of 1812.

Answer: Thaddeus Kosciusko

108

Who was the Gray Ghost?

Clues:

- He was born in 1833 in Virginia.
- He became United States Consul to Hong Kong.
- He was a scout, special aide, and courier for Jeb Stuart.
- He received more compliments and commendations from General Robert E. Lee than any other officer in the Confederate Army.
- With only nine men, he was once able to "stampede 3,000 Union troops."
- After Lee's surrender, he was the only Confederate officer in Virginia excluded from parole.
- His 43rd Battalion Virginia Cavalry was better known as "Rangers."

Answer: John Mosby

Scientists

109

Who helped discover the element used throughout the world in treating cancer and other diseases?

Clues:

- She was the first female faculty member in the 650-year history of the Sorbonne.
- She shared the Nobel prize in physics in 1903.
- She and her husband worked together investigating pitchblende.
- In 1911 she received the Nobel prize in chemistry, the first time that the award was made to a person who had already won a Nobel prize.
- The results of her research were later used to explore the secrets of the atom.
- When she visited the United States with her daughters, American women presented her with a gram of radium worth more than $100,000.
- She was recognized as the world's greatest woman scientist.

Answer: Marie Sklodowska Curie

World Leaders

110

What famous figure poisoned his stepbrother and executed his own mother?

Clues:

- He married at the age of 15.
- He ordered the execution of his 13-year-old wife.
- He killed the husband of his third wife, so he could marry her.
- He suffered from bad skin and body odor.
- He lowered taxes, established old-age pensions, and showered the poor with benefits.
- He spoke two languages.
- He gave live singing performances, with the exits closed so his audience couldn't leave.
- Legend has it that he played a lyre while Rome burned.

Answer: Nero

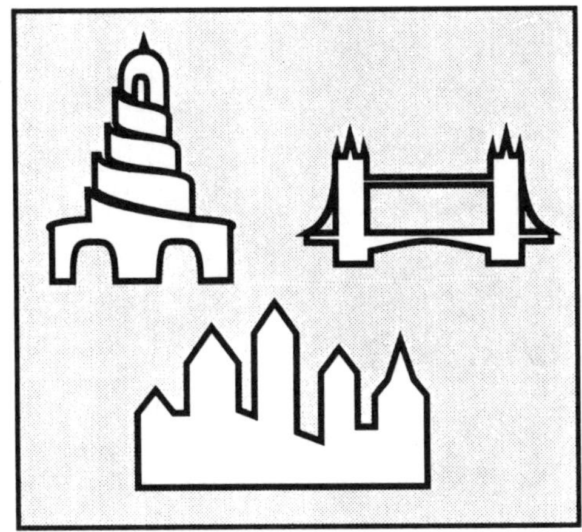

Places

Cities

111

Where can you find the huge granite castle known as the Stony Mountain Fortress?

Clues:

- It is the chief center of its country's industry.
- It has more than 800 bridges.
- It has a great cotton spinning industry.
- It is an important railway center.
- Over half of it was destroyed by American bombers in World War II.
- It is called the Chicago of Japan.
- It has also been called the Japanese Venice because of the many canals, rivers, and arms of the sea that cut through it.
- It is near the eastern entrance of the Inland Sea.

Answer: Osaka, Japan

Countries

112

Where do oil imports cost almost 30 million dollars a day?

Clues:

- Its name is supposedly derived from the red dyewoods to be obtained there.
- It has more land under cultivation than Europe has.
- It is trying to make 80 percent of its autos run on alcohol made from its own sugar cane.
- Seventy percent of its people are crowded within 100 miles of the coast.
- There is an opera house in its jungle.
- More than 90 percent of the people are Catholic.
- It is the most populous nation in Latin America.

Answer: Brazil

113

In what country do families receive a yearly allowance for every child under age 16?

Clues:

- Nearly 1/5 of this country is marshland.
- It has 55,000 lakes.
- Two of its main exports are paper and furniture.
- The inhabitants are thought to have originally come from Central Asia.
- Summers are short but warm. Winters are long, cold, and snowy.
- The northern part of this country lies within the Arctic Circle.
- The basic unit of currency is the markka.
- This country's most well-known gift to the world is the sauna bath.

Answer: Finland

114

Where have horses run free since Roman times?

Clues:

- Another region of this place reigns as the floral-oil capital of the world.
- The people who live here call it "the beautiful, the sweet."
- On the farms they grow everything from wheat to artichokes and cauliflower.
- Cork is harvested on an island off the mainland.
- Its highest point is almost 16,000 feet above sea level.
- It produces about half as much iron ore as the United States.
- It is known for its vineyards and quality wines.

Answer: France

115

Where does one village chop icebergs into ice cubes and ship them abroad to chill drinks?

Clues:

- If all the ice here melted, seas would rise 20 feet.
- It is over three times as large as Texas.
- July temperatures average 50 degrees F.
- Sheep raising is the chief farm activity.
- Inhabitants hunt seals, walrus, and foxes and fish for halibut, salmon, and shrimp.
- This place won home rule from Denmark in 1979.
- Eric the Red founded a colony here in A.D. 982.
- It lies under an icecap that is two miles thick in places.

Answer: Greenland

116

Where did a conqueror and 10,000 of his men enter into a mass marriage with 10,000 local brides?

Clues:

- The first roses bloomed here.
- Some believe that the game of chess originated here.
- It is a mountainous plateau country.
- Uninhabitated deserts cover 38,000 square miles.
- Summer temperatures can rise to 115 degrees F.
- Eighty-five percent of the people earn their livelihoods from agriculture, which includes livestock, wheat, barley, rice, corn, cotton, and melons.
- The highest point is over 18,000 feet above sea level.
- It is the home of the first great highway builder.
- Astronomy grew as a science here.
- The New Year is celebrated on the first day of spring.

Answer: Iran (the conqueror was Alexander the Great)

Lakes and Seas

117

What has been called the "Hoodoo Sea"?

Clues:

- It has been known for at least 100 years.
- It's largest victim was the Cyclops.
- December 5th was a bad day for three victims.
- Scientists researching there observed waterspouts that resembled "wet tornadoes."
- Some sources say that since 1854 that more than 50 ships and aircraft have vanished in or near the area while other sources claim over 100 since 1945.
- It covers about 440,000 square miles.
- It has even been suggested this is the site of the lost continent of Atlantis.
- It is also called "Devil's Triangle."

Answer: Bermuda Triangle

118

What is the world's highest navigable lake?

Clues:

- The Indians still hold that one of its islands is a sacred place.
- It's an 800 feet deep inland sea 138 miles long and 69 miles wide.
- It's named for the amazing swimming wildcats that live on rocky islands and paddle to the mainland for food.
- The lake's shape from the air resembles a wildcat crouched to leap.
- It is supposed to be the home of a monster that resembles a huge seal.
- Jacques-Yves Cousteau, while making an underwater survey, discovered toads two feet long that have evolved to breathe underwater.
- The lake is half in one country and half in another.

Answer: Lake Titicaca

States

119

Where are 80 percent of the known trumpeter swans in the world to be found?

Clues:

- The record high temperature was 100 degrees F. The record low temperature was -80 degrees F.
- The most snowfall in one area was 974.5 inches in one year.
- It has had earthquakes registering 8.4 and 8.6 on the Richter scale.
- Because of its placement on the 180th meridian, it boasts both the easternmost and westernmost points of its country.
- Seventy-pound cabbages and 30-pound turnips grow here.
- One of its glaciers is almost as large as Delaware and Rhode Island combined.
- Captain James Cook explored there in 1778.
- It was purchased for $7.2 million.

Answer: Alaska

120

Where was it so wild that an undertaker advertised group-rate burials for Saturday killings.

Clues:

- The U.S. Government owns over 1/3 of its lands.
- It is here that the Department of Agriculture preserves seeds in concrete vaults from nearly every food plant we know.
- Anasazi farmed here as early as the time of Christ.
- President Grant walked on silver bricks from the street to his hotel when visting here (silver being used instead of gold because gold was so common in the area).
- With part of a foot in this state, you can also be standing in three other states at the same time.
- NORAD (North American Aerospace Defense Command) is centered 1,200 feet below ground here.
- It is called the Centennial State.

Answer: Colorado

121

Where was the first telescoping fishing rod made?

Clues:

- The inventor made it so that he could hide it when he went fishing on the Sabbath.
- Tobacco is grown here.
- In early days in one of its towns a child over 16 years of age could be put to death for cursing a parent.
- The first football tackling dummy was produced there.
- The first American woman to win a patent on an invention lived there.
- The first American-made steel fishhook came from there.
- It gained its nickname from peddlers selling fake nutmegs carved from wood instead of the spice.
- It produced the first copper coins in the United States.
- Its name means "long tidal river."
- Eli Whitney manufactured his cotton gins there.
- It is the third smallest state.

Answer: Connecticut

122

Where is there a city with red lines on the sidewalks marking the Freedom Trail?

Clues:

- Forests cover some 70 percent of the land.
- A historic armory has made guns and ammunition here for our soldiers since George Washington's time.
- Most of the paper for our dollar bills is manufactured here.
- It is thought that Leif Ericson may have visited here about the year A.D. 1000.
- Basketball was born here at a YMCA school and peach baskets were used for the game.
- America's oldest college is located here.
- It produces more cranberries than any other state.
- The mayflower is the state flower.

Answer: Massachusetts

123

What place includes the area explorers called "Dead Man's Journey"?

Clues:

- Ancient seas washed over this land again and again.
- This place had volcanic activity.
- Human beings have lived here for thousands of years.
- Elk, marmots, mountain lions, quail, and pheasants hide away on the slopes and in the woods.
- The historic Palace of the Governors was built by the Spanish 300 years ago.
- Its capital sits at the foot of a mountain range and is 7,000 feet above sea level.
- Only four states claim more land area.
- Forty-seven percent of the nation's uranium is mined here.
- The first atomic test bomb went off in the desert here.

Answer: New Mexico

124

Where was the biggest horse race in the world?

Clues:

- More than 50,000 people won this race.
- The race took place September 16, 1893.
- There are annual rattlesnake roundups here.
- You will find this place in *The Grapes of Wrath*.
- Its name comes from two Choctaw words.
- It was one place where Custer won.
- The capital city covers 649 square miles.
- It is one of the leading wheat producing states.
- More than 60 different Indian tribes live there.

Answer: Oklahoma

125

Which New England state had more cows than people until 1963?

Clues:

- It would be hard to find a place in the United States that has been fought over more in our wars.
- It does not border the sea, but one county is almost entirely surrounded by water.
- The first horse breed developed in America originated here.
- An old saying says this state has nine months snow and three months poor sledding.
- Its most famous product traces its origins back 350 million years.
- It has no city with more than 50,000 people.
- It is known for its sugar bush.

Answer: Vermont

126

What has a nickname that comes from the homes of some of its inhabitants in the 1830s and 1840s?

Clues:

- There the glaciers moved south and parted at Timms Hill and Rib Mountain (or Hill), leaving an island of land.
- If you spear fish there you might catch a sturgeon weighing as much as 150 pounds.
- Forests cover almost half of it.
- A one-time governor said, "Speak to a cow as you would to a lady, because a cow is the foster mother of the human race."
- At times in its history it was a part of the Northwest Territory, a part of Indiana Territory, a part of Illinois Territory, and a part of Michigan Territory.
- It is a land of lakes.
- It has first place in the production of milk and cheese in the United States.

Answer: Wisconsin

Tourist Attractions

127

What was known as "The Devil's Island of America"?

Clues:

- It was named by Juan Manuel de Ayala in 1775.
- It's a 12-acre island of solid rock.
- We know it as the "Island of Pelicans."
- Everything on the island had to be imported.
- Of the total island inhabitants, seven were shot, one drowned, and five went missing and were never found.
- It was the "dark hole" from 1933-1963.
- It has been used as a fortress, a Civil War military prison, a federal penitentiary, and a site of an American Indian occupation.
- It is one of the most popular attractions in the San Francisco Bay area.

Answer: Alcatraz

128

What is the world's bloodiest acre?

Clues:

- Pope Gregory XIV squeezed one handful of its soil and it dripped blood.
- It was cracked by an earthquake in A.D. 422.
- It is four stories high not counting the basements.
- Its 50,000 seats were of marble and stone.
- It was built by Emperor Vespasian.
- The opening celebration given by Titus lasted 100 days.
- 5,000 animals were slaughtered during those 100 days.
- It is also called the Flavian Amphitheater.

Answer: The Colosseum

129

What had a skin of polished limestone?

Clues:
- The limestone was stripped away to build mosques.
- If the building materials were laid end-to-end, they could stretch from the earth to the moon.
- It was old when Christ was born.
- It covers 13 acres and is 451 feet high.
- Its weight is estimated at 6,848,000 tons.
- Its entrance was concealed by a hinged limestone door.
- It and its two near look-alikes were considered one of the seven wonders of the ancient world.
- From its summit, you can see the Sahara Desert and the Nile.
- It is the most massive stone structure ever erected.

Answer: The Great Pyramid

130

What has been called "the longest cemetery in the world"?

Clues:
- It no longer serves its original purpose.
- It took 700 million man-days of forced labor to build.
- It was built 22 centuries ago.
- It's 3,500 miles long.
- 400,000 workers died in broiling heat, freezing cold, and sandstorms.
- It stretches from the Pacific coast to the gates of Central Asia.
- It was built to keep barbarians from Mongolia out of China.

Answer: The Great Wall of China

131

Where can you have lunch, listen to a string quartet, hear poetry read, see Charles Dickens' kitchen knife, or read a newspaper from abroad?

Clues:

- It has 5,600 employees.
- Admission is free.
- It's a popular tourist attraction of Washington, D.C.
- It was founded by Congress in 1800.
- It operates the U.S. Copyright Office.
- President Jefferson's collection was purchased for $24,000 to replace what was burned by British soldiers.
- It has three buildings, each named for a president.
- It is the world's largest library, but no one can borrow a book from here.

Answer: The Library of Congress

132

What building until recently housed the French Ministry of Finance?

Clues:

- The original building was built as a Gothic fort in the 1100s.
- In the 1300s, it became a royal residence.
- It covers 49 acres.
- You now can rent a portion of it for dinners for up to a maximum of 1,000 persons for $50,000 to $100,000.
- It has survived 20 monarchs, 15 architects changing it, revolutions, fires, and Nazi invaders.
- One part was used as a munitions factory during the Franco-Prussian War in 1870.
- It houses the *Mona Lisa*, *Winged Victory*, and the *Venus de Milo*.
- It is the largest art museum and palace in the world.

Answer: The Louvre

133

What city boasts of 1,000,000 visitors a year and has almost no traffic or crime problems and no noise and water pollution?

Clues:

- Most of the homes are air-conditioned.
- It has two theaters; the stage of one can be turned into a pool of water and the curtain rises from the floor.
- Not long after the city was founded, unions became strong and workmen organized cooperatives.
- It does have a slum section.
- Its sports stadium was built with the understanding that the town government would provide the events free of charge.
- It was built at the mouth of the river Sarno, near Capri.
- No one lives in the city now.

Answer: Pompeii

Other Subjects

Diseases

134

What is the 15th leading cause of death nationwide?

Clues:

- If children below the age of 15 are eliminated from these statistics, it becomes the eighth or ninth cause of death.
- Gangrene is the atrophy of the tissue locally affected.
- It kills 16,000 persons annually.
- It usually results from blockage of the inner hollow space, or lumen, of an organ.
- The illness blocks the body's three defenders against disease—oxygen, antibodies, and white blood cells.
- The tissue affected resembles a worm.
- Examination of the blood will show abnormal numbers of white cells.
- Surgery is its only cure.
- The tissue that becomes involved probably has no function.

Answer: Appendicitis

135

What disease is researched through use of the armadillo?

Clues:

- During the 11th, 12th, and 13th centuries, it was epidemic in Europe.
- It affects the body areas that are cooler than other areas.
- It was known in China, India, and Egypt as early as 2,000 B.C.
- It rarely infects adults except under unusual circumstances.
- The U.S. government has had hospitals at Molokai, Hawaii, and Carville, Louisiana, for its victims.
- G. Armauer Hanson, a Norwegian doctor, discovered the bacillus in 1872.
- Victims at one time had to wear or carry bells so they could be identified and avoided.

Answer: Leprosy

Foods

136

What material has gone aboard American and Soviet space flights and with Sir Edmund Hillary when he conquered Mount Everest?

Clues:

- Cortes introduced it to the European world by bringing its original recipe out of Mexico's royal Aztec court to Spain.
- Montezuma drank 50 goblets of it a day.
- Switzerland makes millions a year by exporting this.
- In 1763, it was so popular in England, that beer and ale makers called for legislation restricting its manufacture.
- It flourishes within 20 degrees of the equator.
- Its seed pods are harvested twice a year for up to 40 years.
- It takes 400 beans to make a pound of this substance.
- Scientific tests prove it usually neither causes nor aggravates acne.
- Melbourne, Australia, made a 4,484 pound, 10-foot-tall Easter egg from this material.

Answer: Chocolate

137

What has been called by some "the most perfect thing in the universe"?

Clues:

- It makes oil and water mix.
- If exposed to a high temperature, it becomes tough and rubbery.
- Seventy-four percent of its weight is water.
- It contains nearly all the known vitamins.
- USDA standards range from AA to C.
- It should be stored cold, broad end up.
- The outside is made of calcium.
- An air cell, or pocket of air, forms after it is laid.

Answer: Egg

138

What product is made only in North America?

Clues:

- Production begins in late winter.
- In Canada, Quebec leads in production.
- Although the raw product can come from about five different species, only one species gives the largest amounts.
- Indians used a hollow log in their collection process.
- There is a 35 to 1 ratio of raw product to finished product.
- It must pass the aproning off test.
- New York and Vermont are the leading states in production.

Answer: Maple syrup

139

What common food item can be poisonous in large doses?

Clues:

- Its mother plant is an evergreen tree.
- The spice is provided by the seed of the tree.
- The tree producing this also produces another spice and is the only plant in the world that produces two spices.
- This second spice is made from the aril that envelopes the large oval seed.
- It has a strong aroma.
- It's used in a vast range of foods from meat stuffings to desserts.
- It is native to the Molucca Islands.

Answer: Nutmeg

140

In the manufacturing of what product must the air be washed and filtered every two minutes?

Clues:

- It takes only four hours to "grow" this product.
- "Seeding" is the most important step in making this product.
- Spaniards eat it for breakfast.
- It is an ancient product in other parts of the world, but didn't reach the United States until the 1940s.
- You can make it at home using an ancient Greek recipe.
- Strawberry is the most popular flavor.
- Joseph Metzger brought it to the United States.
- Because it is more easily digested than milk, it is an excellent food for people with weak digestion and for the aged.

Answer: Yogurt

Games

141

What do some historians believe the curved sticks of pre-Christian era shepherds were used for?

Clues:

- Monarchs, through generations, issued edicts prohibiting it.
- A Hollander, after seeing a painting, claimed the Dutch pioneered it.
- A famous Scottish course came into being about 1552.
- When there are two players, it is called a single.
- Mary, Queen of Scots, was the first woman to play.
- The cups are 4½ inches in diameter.
- Scores can be birdies, bogies, and eagles.
- The lowest score is best.

Answer: Golf

142

What game probably inspired bagatelle, bowling, billiards, golf, and Chinese checkers.

Clues:

- It resulted in one of the least-known defeats ever suffered by the U.S. Navy.
- Aztecs; children of ancient Greece and Rome; and Washington, Jefferson, and John Quincy Adams all played this game.
- Today much of the world's supply comes from five West Virginia plants.
- Millions of game pieces are melted to make items such as draperies, car fenders, reflective-bead highway signs, acid, and oil filters.
- Hardest of the game pieces are the transparent red ones.
- Earliest game pieces were fashioned from pebbles, clay, and even polished nuts.

Answer: Marbles

143

What does the city of Derby, England, claim was originated there in A.D. 217, when the Romans occupied ancient Britain.

Clues:

- It is played on a rectangular field 100 to 120 yards by 55 to 75 yards.
- The team scoring the largest number of goals is the winner.
- When one team violates a rule, the other team gets a free kick at the offender's goal.
- It is played with a round, leather-covered, rubber ball.
- The object of the game is to kick or head butt the ball into a goal net.
- The game is divided into 45-minute halves with a 10-minute interval in between.
- It is one of the most popular sports in the world.
- It is the original version of American football.

Answer: Soccer

144

What may be the world's least expensive competitive sport?

Clues:

- Johnny Unitas is an expert at this sport.
- Filipinos used the equipment for hunting.
- It's known as the Prince of Wales' toy.
- The equipment originated in China.
- A player must have a balanced stance and be able to twist hips or shoulders when necessary.
- The secret of the sport is good wrist action.
- Its name means "come, come."
- In competition, contestants loop-the-loop as many times as possible to break a tie.

Answer: Yo-yo

Metals

145

What never occurs in metallic form in nature, but its compounds are present, to some extent, in almost all rocks, vegetation, and animals?

Clues:

- It takes about 10 kilowatt hours of electricity to produce a pound of this.
- The affinity of this for oxygen makes it difficult to obtain the metal.
- The United States is the world's largest producer.
- A Frenchman's work led to the production of this commercially—a metal that was once more valuable than gold soon was being produced at $17 a pound.
- It was first produced in 1825.
- Its largest uses are in transportation, architecture, and in constructing satellites and spacecrafts.
- It is one of the most abundant metals and the lightest in common use.

Answer: Aluminum

146

What substance is about 21 times as heavy as water?

Clues:

- It was once considered so useless that it was thrown away.
- It was used by Thomas Edison and Wilhelm Roentgen.
- It is recyclable.
- It is found principally in South Africa and the Soviet Union.
- Seventy-five percent of the world's output of this is used by industry.
- It is not damaged by any of the pure acids.
- It is one of the earth's most expensive metals.
- It is used on the best surgical instruments.

Answer: Platinum

Minerals

147

What was thought to protect a warrior in battle, prevent mental illness, and protect the wearer from poison?

Clues:

- It was first discovered in India.
- The automobile industry is the principal buyer of this in the industrial stage.
- It's the only mineral that can be cut and polished in the same operation.
- It's a mineral composed solely of carbon.
- Henry Ford first discovered that, on a large scale, it is the cheapest industrial abrasive for long-term use in spite of its high cost.
- In only one rock, kimberlite, does it occur originally.
- The largest blue one is called Hope.
- It has been a symbol of love since 1477 when Maximilian I of Austria gave one to Mary of Burgundy.

Answer: Diamond

148

What substance has influenced human migrations and conquests since prehistoric times?

Clues:

- It existed before the rock formations of most mountains and the soil of the plains.
- It is employed in industry in the manufacture of glass, pottery, dyes for textiles, and soap.
- Men of primitive tribes traded their wives and children for it.
- Your body couldn't function without it.
- It can be found as two sources.
- In the natural source, it is virtually impermeable.
- Its abandoned mines have been suggested and tested as places to store high-level radioactive wastes.

Answer: Salt

Miscellaneous Subjects

149

What material did the Air Force bombers drop by the tons to frustrate enemy radar during World War II?

Clues:

- It conducts heat and cold.
- It shuts out sunlight.
- It is oilproof, greaseproof, nontoxic, nonabsorptive, and has no taste or odor.
- It begins as a reddish-brown rock.
- It can be twisted, folded, crimped, stapled, welded, and molded into any shape.
- It is used in 98 percent of all American households.
- Coming in different colors, it makes attractive wrap for presents.

Answer: Aluminum foil

150

What community was founded in 1855 by Christian Metz?

Clues:

- It was formed by a German religious sect, founded in 1714.
- It is made up of seven villages and contains 26,000 acres.
- Its denominational name is the "Community of True Inspiration."
- Its members are buried in order of death, not in family groups.
- Its name means "remain true" or "believe faithfully."
- It is the oldest and largest communistic venture on American soil.
- In 1932, many communistic practices were dropped, and all members were issued stock in this profit-sharing society.

Answer: Amana Colonies

151

What is the nickname of the projectile weapon that would probably strike an adversary at 80 yards, might possibly strike at 100, and was essentially inaccurate at longer range?

Clues:

- An army recruit was considered unskilled until he could get off four shots in a minute using this weapon.
- The long one weighed 14 pounds, the weight being necessary to aid thrusting movements with the bayonet as well as making it useful as a club.
- All were made in .75 caliber and were smoothbore to facilitate rapid loading.
- Military tactics at the time stressed rapid fire rather than accuracy.
- It was the chief shoulder weapon of the British Army from early 1700 until 1815.
- Part of its name probably referred to the color of the barrel.
- The 46-inch barrel version was designated the Long Land Musket and the 42-inch barrel model was the Short Land Musket.

Answer: Brown Bess

152

What was the "wonder of the age" in 1869?

Clues:

- Though non-living, he received several write-in votes for local office in the elections of 1869.
- Originally from Fort Dodge, Iowa, this wonder became famous across the nation.
- He was buried in New York.
- He was thought to have died from a stomachache.
- The public was charged $.50 to see him lying in state.
- When he was taken from his grave, a block and tackle were needed to lift him.
- Before being buried, he was covered with sulfuric acid.
- Hull and Newell were involved in this hoax.

Answer: The Cardiff Giant

153

What originally filled a huge room and cost hundreds of thousands of dollars?

Clues:

- They have been credited with saving the life of hundreds of critically ill open-heart surgery patients.
- They are used as a navigation aid on airplanes, ships, and spacecraft and to control machines in factories.
- They may produce drawings and paintings.
- One was designed in 1834 which had all the important features needed, but metalworkers were unable to make the parts precisely enough.
- An important part is made of an element found in sand.
- They are used to store more than 20,000 fingerprints a day by the F.B.I.
- One type uses only the two digits of the binary number systems.

Answer: Computers

154

What cost $300 to be made, but was later offered for sale as salvage?

Clues:

- It was built in London.
- Pass and Stow manufactured it.
- The world's largest radiographic, or X-ray, picture ever made on a single sheet of film is of this.
- It was hidden under the floor of a church for almost a year.
- Farmers in Lehigh County, Pennsylvania, hid it in fear the British would melt it down for bullets.
- It was put on a special railroad flatcar and moved to Boston for the 128th anniversary celebration of the Battle of Bunker Hill.
- It weighs over a ton and has a lip circumference of 12 feet.

Answer: The Liberty Bell

155

What institution has a history dating back more than 6,000 years?

Clues:
- Aristotle had a famous one at his school.
- Julius Caesar made plans for one in Rome, but it was not built until seven years after his death.
- Mt. Vesuvius buried one intact in Herculaneum and the National Museum in Naples has the results.
- According to legend, 70 Jewish scholars were shut in cells until they produced what Ptolemy II wanted for one.
- The most famous one was in Alexandria, Egypt.
- The first public one in the American Colonies was believed to have been built in Newport, Rhode Island, in 1750.
- The one at Harvard University is the oldest in the United States, having been founded in 1638.
- Benjamin Franklin established the first one in the United States run by subscription or dues.

Answer: Libraries

156

What objects were pulverized and used in medicines as recently as the last century?

Clues:
- Their name seems to have originated from an Arabic word meaning "pitch" or "asphalt."
- Herodotus wrote about them in one of his history books.
- Napoleon Bonaparte had scientists make the first systematic survey of these objects.
- Napoleon shipped two of these home for Josephine's drawing room.
- In 1976, one was treated with cobalt-60 radiation in France and then sent home.
- A wealth of information about ancient disease patterns has been learned by studying them.
- They had food and drink, furniture, combs and razors, jewelry, and even gold with them.
- 150 yards of fabric was the minimum, 450 yards was average, and as much as 876 yards was necessary to create one of these.

Answer: Mummies

157

What hangs like a cherry on a stem, weighs only 1/50 of an ounce, and is 85 percent water by weight?

Clues:

- It is pink in color.
- It is the world's most compact and intricate chemical plant.
- It rests in a bony cradle.
- Fertility and life depend on this.
- It was believed to be an organ that secreted waste material from the brain.
- It is the chemical boss of your body.
- It encourages growth and healing.
- Loss of its function can cause dwarfism and sterility.

Answer: Pituitary gland

158

What was first recited during the National School Celebration of October 21, 1892?

Clues:

- It was written in 1892, and James B. Upham is the person most often credited with the original version.
- It was rephrased three times.
- It was conceived as part of a promotion campaign by the magazine *The Youth's Companion.*
- Publishers of the magazine vied to be recognized as its author.
- It received congressional blessing 50 years after it was written.
- The official words were set down at the Second National Flag Conference in 1924.
- This is traditionally recited with a hand over one's heart.

Answer: Pledge of Allegiance (Pledge to the Flag)

159

What is this killer?

Clues:

- One of the earliest occurrences happened in Belgium in 1930, resulting in the deaths of 60 people.
- It also occurred in London during the week of December 5-9, 1952.
- Four thousand people died at that time.
- The greatest fatalities were among the elderly.
- It happened in London again in 1962, but took only 340 lives.
- If you were in London at this time, your mouth would have had a metallic taste.
- It lead to England's Clean Air Act.
- The name derives from a combination of the words "smoke" and "fog."

Answer: Smog

160

What is the most powerful drying agent known?

Clues:

- It is poisonous.
- Its source, at one time, grew only in Asia.
- Its source is now grown in Florida, Georgia, Louisiana, Mississippi, and Texas.
- It is obtained from nuts (or seeds) of a tree.
- It is used in printing ink, waterproof fabrics, and paper.
- High-grade, quick-drying varnishes, lacquers, and enamels use it as an ingredient.
- It is sometimes called China wood oil.

Answer: Tung oil

Natural Phenomena

161

What is the mountain range that was seen by Robert Peary in 1896?

Clues:

- It was 400 miles west of the northern tip of Greenland.
- Although Peary saw it, Donald MacMillan accurately identified it.
- This may have been why scholars of the Middle Ages were deceived into thinking that the earth was flat.
- A different form of this may have led the Vikings.
- It is one of the most spectacular *fata morgana* known to science.
- The mountain range was caused by bending light.
- It is an optical illusion.

Answer: Mirage

162

What are the "macaronis" that are found in the caves of the Cro-Magnon men?

Clues:

- One ancient Chinese manuscript interprets them as omens of imminent battle; while in the Arctic regions, they were often believed to be spirits of the dead, specifically suicides or those killed in battle.
- They cause numerous unnecessary fire alarms.
- They occur all the time, but are most likely to be seen in September, October, March, and April.
- They are caused by electrons and protons shot out from the sun.
- They sometimes cause electrical blackouts.
- Unlike rainbows, they appear in only one or two colors—red and green.
- They usually take place about 70 miles above the earth's surface and are several hundred miles high.

Answer: The Northern Lights (Aurora Borealis)

Resources

Allen, John. *One Hundred Great Lives*. New York: Greystone Press, 1945.

American Heritage. *Men of Science and Invention*. New York: Harper & Row, 1960.

American Heritage (Magazines). Eight issues a year. New York: American Heritage.

The Annals of America. 24 vol. Chicago: Encyclopaedia Britannica, 1968 (a new edition is available).

Associated Press. *The Sports Immortals*. Englewood Cliffs, NJ: Prentice-Hall, 1972.

Audubon Nature Encyclopedia. 12 vol. Philadelphia: Curtis Publishing,1964.

Boys' Life (Magazines). Irving, TX: Boy Scouts of America.

Brownstone, David, and Irene Franck. *People in the News*. New York: Macmillan, 1993.

Changing Times (Magazines). Editors Park, MD: Changing Times.

Colliers Encyclopedia. 24 vol. New York: Macmillan, 1991.

Compton's Encyclopedia. 26 vol. Chicago: Encyclopaedia Britannica, 1992.

Costain, Thomas B. *The Chord of Steel*. Garden City, NY: Doubleday, 1960.

Current Biography Year Books. Bronx, NY: H. W. Wilson.

Davis, Mac. *100 Greatest Sports Feats*. New York: Grosset and Dunlap, 1964.

Dickinson, Mary B. *National Geographic Picture Atlas of Our World*. rev. ed. Washington, DC: National Geographic Society, 1993.

Dictionary of American History. rev. ed. 6 vol. New York: Scribner, 1976.

Encyclopaedia Britannica. *Discovering Natural Science*. Chicago: Encyclopaedia Britannica, 1971.

Encyclopedia Americana. 30 vol. Danbury, CT: Grolier, 1993.

Encyclopedia of World Travel. 3d rev. ed. 2 vol. Garden City, NY: Doubleday, 1979.

Evans, Ivor, ed. *Brewer's Dictionary of Phrase and Fable*, 14th ed. New York: HarperCollins, 1989.

Field & Stream (Magazines). Boulder, CO: Field & Stream.

Ford Times (Magazines). Dearborn, MI: Ford Motor Co.

Golden Book Encyclopedia of Natural Science. 16 vol. New York: Golden Press, 1962.

Good Housekeeping (Magazines). Red Oak, IA: Good Housekeeping.

Grolier Library of North American Biographies. 10 vol. Danbury, CT: Grolier, 1994.

Hoffman, Mark S., ed. *World Almanac and Book of Facts, 1994*. Mahwah, NJ: World Almanac, 1993.

Illustrated Encyclopedia of the Animal Kingdom. 20 vol. Danbury, CT: Danbury Press, 1972.

Johnston, Mary. *Roman Life*. Chicago: Scott Foresman, 1957.

Ladies Home Journal (Magazines). Des Moines, IA: Ladies Home Journal.

Leach, Maria, and Jerome Fried, eds. *Funk and Wagnall's Standard Dictionary of Folklore, Mythology and Legend*. San Francisco: Harper SF, 1984.

Lincoln Library of Sports Champions. 20 vol. Chicago: Encyclopaedia Britannica, 1989.

Mac Globe (Computer Software). Novato, CA: Broderbund Software, 1992.

Macdonald, David. *The Encyclopedia of Mammals*. Equinox (Oxford), 1984.

Marshall Cavendish International Wildlife Encyclopedia. 24 vols. New York: Marshall Cavendish, 1988.

Menke, Frank G. *The Encyclopedia of Sports*. New York: A. S. Barnes, 1969.

Miers, Earl Schenck. *America and Its Presidents*. New York: Grosset & Dunlap, 1982.

National Geographic (Magazines). Washington, DC: National Geographic Society.

National Geographic. *Those Inventive Americans*. Washington, DC: National Geographic Society, 1971.

National Geographic World (Magazines). Washington, DC: National Geographic Society.

National Wildlife (Magazines). Vienna, VA: National Wildlife Membership Services.

Natural History (Magazines). Harlan, IA: Natural History.

The New Book of Popular Science. 6 vol. Danbury, CT: Grolier, 1987.

The New Grolier Electronic Encyclopedia (CD-ROM). Danbury, CT: Grolier, 1991.

Outdoor Life (Magazines). Boulder, CO: Outdoor Life.

Perrins, Christopher, and Alex L. A. Middleton. *Encyclopedia of Birds*. New York: Facts on File, 1985.

Peterson, Roger Tory. *A Field Guide to the Birds: East of the Rockies*. 4th ed. New York: Houghton Mifflin, 1980.

Petzal, David E. *Encyclopedia of Sporting Firearms*. New York: Facts on File, 1991.

Pictorial Encyclopedia People Who Made America. 20 vol. Skokie, IL: United States History Society, 1973.

Popular Mechanics (Magazines). Red Oak, IA: Popular Mechanics.

Popular Science (Magazines). Boulder, CO: Popular Science.

The Random House Dictionary of the English Language. 2d unabridged edition. New York: Random, 1987.

Ranger Rick's Nature Magazine (Magazines). Vienna, VA: National Wildlife Federation.

Reader's Digest (Magazines). Pleasantville, NY: Reader's Digest.

Robbins, Chandler, Bertel Bruun, and Herbert S. Zim. *Birds of North America: A Guide to Field Identification*. New York: Golden Press, 1983.

Sedeen, Margaret, ed. *National Geographic Picture Atlas of Our Fifty States*. Washington, DC: National Geographic Society, 1991.

Seventeen (Magazines). Radnor, PA: Seventeen.

Smithsonian (Magazines). Boulder, CO: Smithsonian.

The Software Toolworks World Atlas. CD ROM. Novato, CA: Software Toolworks, 1991.

Sport (Magazines). Los Angeles: Peterson Publishing.

Sports Illustrated (Magazines). weekly. Tampa, FL: Sports Illustrated.

Sullivan, George. *More "How Do They Make It?"* Philadelphia: Westminster, 1969.

Time Table of History—Science and Innovation. (CD-ROM). Novato, CA: Software Toolworks, 1991.

U.S. History on CD ROM. Parsippany, NJ: Bureau Development, 1991.

Webster's New Biographical Dictionary. Springfield, MA: Merriam-Webster, 1983.

Webster's Tenth New Collegiate Dictionary. Springfield, MA: Merriam-Webster, 1993.

Wild, Wild World of Animals (Series). Alexandria, VA: Time-Life Films, 1977.

World Book Encyclopedia. rev. ed. 22 vol. Chicago: World Book,1993.

Zim, Herbert, and Alexander C. Martin. *Flowers: A Guide to Familiar American Wildflowers*. New York: Golden Press, 1950.

Zimmerman, J. E. *Dictionary of Classical Mythology*. New York: Bantam Books, 1983.

Zoobooks. (Series). Wildlife Education, 1980.

Subject Index

Please note that numbers listed are not page numbers but question numbers.